The Mason Jar COOKIE COOKBOOK

LONNETTE PARKS

SQUAREONE
PUBLISHERS

Cover Designer: Phaedra Mastrocola
Cover Photo: Gary A. Rosenberg
Typesetter: Gary A. Rosenberg
Editor: Joanne Abrams

Square One Publishers
Garden City Park, NY 11040
(516) 535-2010 • www.squareonepublishers.com

Library of Congress Cataloging-in-Publication Data

Parks, Lonnette.
   The mason jar cookie cookbook : how to create mason jar cookie mixes /
Lonnette Parks.
    p. cm.
  ISBN 0-7570-0046-0
  1. Cookies. I. Title.
  TX772 .P29 2002
  641.8′654—dc21

                        2002006224

Printed in the United States of America

10 9 8 7 6

Contents

Cookie Recipes

Brownie and Bar Recipes

Introduction

Have you ever walked into a country store and been delighted by rows of beautiful Mason jar mixes? Decorated with a square of fabric and a brightly colored ribbon, each container holds the nonperishable ingredients—flour, sugar, and the like—needed to bake a batch of luscious cookies. All you have to do is follow the simple instructions on the attached card, and you have a batch of home-baked treats. No fuss. No bother. Just delicious cookies.

If you have wished that you could make these Mason jar mixes in your own home, or if you have tasted Mason jar cookies and wished you could bake them yourself, I have wonderful news: You don't have to be Martha Stewart to create these charming, practical gifts. Nor do you have to be an expert to bake treats that will delight adult and child alike. In fact, *The Mason Jar Cookie Cookbook* was designed specifically to bring the pleasures of home-baked cookies not only into your home, but also into the homes of friends and family. In these pages, you'll find fifty recipes for truly delectable cookies—treats like Best Ever Chocolate Chip Cookies, Gooey Turtle Bars, and Mocha Rum Balls. These cookies are easy to make for even the novice cook, and are guaranteed to please the most demanding of cookie monsters. Better yet, this book will show you how to assemble beautiful Mason jar cookie mixes so that you can give the gift of home baking to everyone on your list, from your child's teacher to your next-door neighbor to your favorite hostess. I have been making Mason jar cookie mixes for years, and I can tell you that *everyone's* face lights up when they see these mixes. That's why they're not just perfect gifts, but also fund-raising favorites. Who can resist a beautifully arranged container that holds nearly everything needed to bake rich, chocolatey brownies or old-fashioned sugar cookies? All the lucky recipient has to do is pour the contents of the jar into a bowl, add a few basic ingredients like butter and eggs, and follow a handful of easy instructions. The result? Wonderful homemade cookies in minutes!

The Mason Jar Cookie Cookbook begins by discussing cookie basics. The first part of the "Basics" chapter guides you in buying the best ingredients and equipment for your baking adventures, and provides tips for mixing, forming, and baking scrumptious cookies. Here, you'll find invaluable advice that will help you turn out perfect cookies every time. The second part of the chapter covers all the ins and outs of creating the jars. What size jar should you use? How can you make neat, even layers of ingredients? And how can you add those finishing touches that turn the jar into a beautiful gift? This chapter tells all.

Following the "Basics" chapter are fifty recipes for luscious cookies, brownies, and bars. Because this book is designed for both the baker *and* the crafter, you'll find that each recipe has been presented in a unique two-page spread. Intended for the home baker, the left-hand page contains the recipe itself. Kitchen-tested, each recipe is simple to follow and yields simply scrumptious results. Intended for the crafter, the right-hand page provides directions for creating the jarred mix. In each case, a diagram shows you how to layer the ingredients for attractive results, and a box neatly displays the baking instructions you'll want to include on your gift tag.

So take out your mixing bowl and get ready to experience the joys of Mason jar cookies. Whether you want to fill your kitchen with the aroma of homemade cookies, you'd like to give distinctive Mason jar mixes to cookie-loving friends and family, or you're searching for a unique fund-raising idea, you're sure to find what you want within these pages. Who knows? You may even bring home-baked cookies back in style.

The**Basics**

Welcome to the world of Mason jar cookies! This book will show you just how easy it is to bake up a perfect batch of cookies—truly scrumptious treats like Blondies, Cranberry Cream Drops, and Death by Chocolate Cookies. Just as important, *The Mason Jar Cookie Cookbook* will guide you in making beautiful Mason jar mixes that will bring the gift of home baking to friends who simply love homemade cookies (and who doesn't?), but who *think* they don't have the time to whip up a batch on their own. (They'll be happy to learn that they're wrong!)

While Mason jar cookie mixes—and the cookies themselves—are a snap to make, you'll enjoy the best results if you keep a few guidelines in mind as you select ingredients, create your cookie jar mixes, and turn your mixes into wonderful home-baked cookies. This chapter provides all the basics, insuring that both your cookie mixes and your cookies are the best they can be.

INGREDIENTS

All of the ingredients used in the *The Mason Jar Cookie Cookbook* are common, easy-to-find items. While a few of the ingredients, such as wheat germ, are used in only one or two recipes, many, such as flour and sugar, are used in most or all of the recipes in the book. Because these products are so important to the success of your cookies, let's take a few minutes to learn more about them so that you can choose the best ingredients possible for your baked goods.

Flour

If stored carelessly, flour can absorb moisture, affecting the outcome of your Mason jar cookies. To keep your flour at its freshest, store it in a clean airtight container, and place the container in a cool place.

All of the recipes in this book call for all-purpose flour, which is a blend of refined hard and soft wheat flours. Choose either bleached or unbleached flour for your cookies, as either one will produce delicious results. The difference is only that the latter type has not undergone a bleaching process, and so contains more vitamin E than its bleached counterpart.

Once opened, flour will stay fresh for up to six months. Simply keep it in a clean, airtight container that prevents the product from absorbing any moisture, and store it in a cool place.

Granulated Sugar

Whenever the word "sugar" is used in this book, the recipe calls for granulated white sugar—although you may also use a super-granulated (superfine) sugar, which is a finer grind that is still coarse enough to have easily discernible crystals. White sugar is generally the sweetener of choice when a crisp cookie is desired or when you want to enhance sweetness without adding the molasses-like flavor of brown sugar.

Store your sugar as you would store flour—in a clean, airtight container kept in a cool place.

Brown Sugar

Brown sugar is simply granulated white sugar that has been coated with a film of molasses, and so is more flavorful than its white counterpart. When making your Mason jar cookies, use either light or dark brown sugar—the choice is yours. Just be aware that in addition to being darker in color, dark brown sugar has a more pronounced flavor than light.

Because brown sugar is moister than white sugar, the resulting cookies will tend to be delightfully chewy. Be aware, though, that the same moisture which makes brown sugar so irresistible also makes it prone to turn hard and lumpy. To keep your purchase from turning into a rock-hard mass, be sure to store it in an airtight container (doubled zip-lock plastic bags are great) and to keep it in a cool place. If the sugar should become hard, however, simply microwave it, uncovered, for twenty to thirty seconds, or until it becomes soft enough to use with ease.

If, despite all precautions, your brown sugar turns hard, don't panic—and don't toss it out. Just heat the sugar in a microwave oven for twenty to thirty seconds, and it will become soft enough to use with ease.

Eggs

Eggs help provide the structural framework for cookies, allowing them to rise and puff. For best results when making the recipes in this book, use eggs marked "large" and buy the freshest ones you can find. Then refrigerate them and use them before the expiration date.

To keep fat and cholesterol under control, many people now use egg substitutes when cooking and baking. However, while egg substitutes can be used in some baked goods, they will not work well in Mason jar cookies, as the dough they produce is crumbly and dry. For moist and delicious results, always choose the freshest whole eggs when following the recipes in this book.

Butter

For the best flavor and texture, use only the freshest, sweetest butter in your Mason jar cookies.

For the best flavor and texture, I use only pure sweet (unsalted) butter in my recipes. If you prefer, you may substitute margarine for the butter, but don't use light butter, light margarine, or diet spreads, as all of these products contain added moisture that will adversely affect the finished cookies.

You'll find that the recipes in this book usually express butter amounts in terms of cups ($\frac{1}{2}$ cup, $\frac{1}{4}$ cup, etc.). These amounts are very easy to measure, as one stick of butter ($\frac{1}{4}$ pound) equals $\frac{1}{2}$ cup, or eight tablespoons. Usually, the recipe's ingredients list specifies the use of softened butter. To soften the butter, simply allow it to sit at room temperature for about forty-five minutes or until it's soft enough to cream easily with a fork, but not runny. Don't leave it out of the refrigerator too long, as overly soft butter will result in excessive spreading during the baking process. In fact, butter that is either too warm *or* too cold can actually alter the temperature of the cookie dough, affecting baking times.

Butter can be stored in either the refrigerator or the freezer. Kept in the refrigerator, butter remains fresh for up to two weeks; in the freezer, for up to six months.

Baking Soda and Baking Powder

The majority of the Mason jar cookie recipes contain one or both of two common forms of leavening—baking soda and baking powder.

Also called bicarbonate of soda and sodium bicarbonate, baking soda is a naturally occurring substance. When used alone, baking soda has no leavening power. However, when used in a cookie batter that also contains an acidic ingredient such as molasses or buttermilk, the cookies rise, producing a tender crumb.

Baking powder is a mixture of baking soda and other ingredients, the most important of which is an acidic compound such as cream of tartar. When this product is mixed in a batter with wet ingredients, leavening occurs. No acidic ingredients are needed, as the acid is already in the powder.

Why do the recipes in this book sometimes use one of these products and sometimes use both? Clearly, when no acidic ingredient is used in the batter, baking powder is the leavening of choice. But other factors also come into play. For instance, baking powder is most appropriate when lighter colored, puffier cookies are desired. And baking soda can be used to lend a somewhat salty flavor to baked products.

Both baking soda and baking powder are inexpensive and readily available. Stored in covered containers, they will remain fresh and potent for up to six months.

Flavored Extracts

Although the occasional recipe in this book uses almond or lemon extract, most of the cookies are flavored with vanilla extract. In prepar-

Imitation extracts often leave a bitter aftertaste. Instead of saving a few cents by purchasing an artificial product, buy only pure extracts, and enjoy true vanilla, lemon, and almond flavor.

ing your Mason jar cookie recipes, try to use only those products labelled "pure." Imitation extracts are composed of artificial ingredients, and often have a bitter aftertaste. These products can be used, of course, but since a bottle of extract lasts a long time, it makes sense to spend a little more and buy the best.

Oatmeal

In *The Mason Jar Cookie Cookbook,* oatmeal is used in a variety of recipes to add a distinctive yet subtle flavor and a wonderfully chewy texture. I use quick-cooking oats in my cookie recipes, as I find that they produce the best results. This product will stay fresh for up to six months when stored in a clean airtight container.

Nuts

Due to their oil content, nuts are a highly perishable ingredient. Unless you bake often, buy nuts in small amounts and store any leftovers in the refrigerator or freezer.

The Mason jar cookie recipes use a variety of nuts—including walnuts, pecans, peanuts, macadamia nuts, and almonds—to add flavor and crunch to baked goods. Feel free to replace one type of nut with another, according to your preferences. However, whenever the recipe specifies almonds, it is suggested that you avoid substituting other nuts simply because almonds have such a special and distinctive flavor—one that cannot be replaced by any other nut.

The flavor of nuts is carried by their essential oils, which is the same component that makes all nuts perishable. If you buy nuts in shells, they'll stay fresher, as the shells will protect them from air, moisture, heat, and light. In fact, unshelled nuts can be stored for about twice as long as shelled nuts. If the nuts are already shelled, though, place them in an airtight container and keep the container in a cool, dry, dark place for up to two months before using. To increase the nuts' shelf life, place the container in the refrigerator, where they'll stay fresh for up to four months, or in the freezer, where they can remain for up to six months.

Baking Chips

Baking chips add color, creaminess, and flavor to cookies. A variety of chips are used in this book, including butterscotch, peanut butter, vanilla, white chocolate (which contains no chocolate at all), and chocolate. In each of these cases, you will, of course, get the best results when you opt for the highest-quality product available, but this is especially true when selecting chocolate chips. I always use the purest chocolate chips—never chips that are labelled "imitation" chocolate. Although a bit more pricey, pure chocolate chips result in a truer chocolate flavor as well as a creamier texture.

> Like imitation extracts, imitation chocolate chips do not deliver the best flavor. To insure that your Blondies, S'More Bars, and other treats taste as good as they look, use only pure chocolate chips.

If you use only a portion of a bag of chocolate chips, be sure to wrap the remaining chips tightly and store them in a cool (60°F to 70°F), dry place. If kept in a warm environment, the chocolate may develop pale gray steaks and blotches as the cocoa butter rises to the surface. In damp conditions, the chocolate may even form tiny gray sugar crystals on the surface. In either case, the chocolate can still be used, but both the flavor and the texture will be slightly affected. Note that because of the milk solids found in both milk and white chocolate, these chips should be stored for no longer than nine months. Semisweet and bittersweet chocolate, though, can remain fresh for up to *ten years* when properly stored.

BASIC COOKIE-MAKING EQUIPMENT

Only the simplest of kitchen equipment is needed to bake delicious Mason jar cookies. The following items will make baking an easier, more pleasurable activity, and will help you enjoy success each and every time you select a recipe from this book.

Measuring Cups and Spoons

Be sure to use nested metal or plastic cups to measure dry ingredients, and graduated glass or plastic cups to measure liquids. Never use liquid measuring cups for flour, as you could end up adding an extra tablespoon or more per cup!

The accurate measuring of ingredients is essential to baking success whether preparing Mason jar cookies or making any other home-baked treat. And the key to accurate measuring is the use of basic measuring cups and spoons.

When measuring dry ingredients such as flour, sugar, and oatmeal, always use dry measuring cups. Available in sets that usually include 1-cup, ½-cup, ⅓-cup, and ¼-cup measures, these cups allow you to spoon or scoop up the ingredient and then level it off with a straight edge—a metal spatula or knife—for greatest accuracy. *Never* use a liquid measuring cup for this purpose as it will make precise measuring impossible.

When measuring liquid ingredients such as milk, applesauce, or melted butter, be sure to use liquid measuring cups, which are clear cups with markings that indicate ¼-, ⅓-, ½-, ⅔-, and ¾-cup levels. For greatest accuracy, place the cup on the counter and bend down to check the amount at eye level.

Always use measuring spoons—not the teaspoons and tablespoons you use to set your table—to measure small amounts of spices and the like. These inexpensive tools come in sets that usually include 1-table-poon, 1-teaspoon, $1/2$-teaspoon, and $1/4$-teaspoon measures. When using dry ingredients, if possible, dip the spoon in the container until it over-flows, and then shake the spoon to level it off. When measuring wet ingredients, pour the liquid until it reaches the top edge of the spoon.

Mixing Bowls

When preparing the dough for your Mason jar cookies, you'll need just a few different mixing bowls. A small bowl of about 1 quart in size will be called for just occasionally to hold a sugary topping or another sin-gle ingredient. More commonly, you'll want a medium-sized bowl (about 2 quarts) and a large bowl (about 3 quarts). This simple equip-ment will give you the room you need to cream the butter, mix the dry ingredients, and ultimately combine all of the ingredients together—without making a floury mess on the kitchen counter.

Mixing bowls can be made of a variety of materials, including glass, stainless steel, plastic, and ceramic. If you don't already own a set of bowls, consider buying tempered glass. Glass bowls not only allow you to easily see when the ingredients are well mixed, but also make it pos-sible to microwave ingredients such as chocolate.

Baking Sheets

Every baker has personal preferences regarding baking sheets. I feel that I get the best results with air cushion sheets, which are made of two layers of metal with a "layer" of air in between. The dual layered sheets allow air to better circulate under the cookie-baking surface, reducing hot spots so that cookies bake beautifully all across the sheet, and not

Mixing bowls can be made of a variety of materials, including stainless steel, glass, ceramic, and plastic. While all of these are good choices, nonmetal dishes allow you to microwave ingredients directly in the bowl—a real advantage when a recipe directs you to melt chocolate before adding it to the cookie dough.

Composed of two sheets of metal with a layer of air in between, air cushion baking sheets reduce hot spots so that cookies bake beautifully all across the sheet.

Whenever a recipe directs you to grease your cookie sheet, a great alternative is to line it with baker's parchment paper. Available in supermarkets and specialty stores, this paper not only prevents sticking, but also saves on clean-up time.

just in the middle. These sheets come with both nonstick and regular surfaces. Either surface will yield great results.

To insure even baking, use a cookie sheet that fits in the oven with at least one inch to spare around each edge. Whether or not your sheet is nonstick, it is not necessary to grease the baking surface unless it is called for in the recipe. When greasing is recommended, simply use a piece of paper toweling to rub a small amount of butter or other shortening evenly over the bottom and sides of the pan. A small amount of cooking spray may also be used.

Electric Mixers

While an electric mixer is by no means a cookie-baking necessity, if you do have one on hand, it will make quick work of creaming the butter, and in some cases can also be used to combine the wet ingredients with the dry. Either a portable (hand-held) or a stationary (stand) mixer can be used—although I personally like a portable model. If you don't have a mixer, just use a sturdy wooden spoon and a little elbow grease. Your cookies will be just as delicious.

Baking Racks

Most of the recipes in this book direct you to first cool the baked cookies on the pan for five minutes, and then transfer the cookies to a baking rack for further cooling. Made of wire, these racks speed the cooling process by allowing air to flow around both the tops and bottoms of the cookies. In most cases, your Mason jar creations will be ready for serving or storage within twenty minutes.

If you don't own cooling racks, you can, of course, simply transfer the cookies directly from the baking sheet to a plate. Be aware, though, that the moisture from the hot cookies may make your baked goods slightly adhere to the plate. Once the cookies have cooled, be sure to lift them carefully to avoiding breakage.

MAKING THE COOKIES

The recipes in this book are easy to follow for even the beginning baker. Just keep a few simple guidelines in mind, and you're sure to bake mouth-watering cookies each and every time you select a Mason jar cookie recipe.

Measuring the Ingredients

Earlier in the chapter, I mentioned the importance of accurately measuring cookie dough ingredients. (See page 12.) In addition to following the basic guidelines presented in that discussion, keep these tips in mind when preparing your Mason jar cookie dough.

❏ There's no need to sift the flour before—or after—measuring it for your Mason jar cookies. But keep in mind that the amount of flour used is crucial, so care should be taken to avoid adding more flour than recommended. To keep the flour light and the measurement true, either dip the cup in the flour bin or spoon the flour into the cup before leveling with a straight edge, such as a spatula or knife.

❏ When measuring honey, molasses, peanut butter, or any other sticky ingredient, remember to grease the cup first, as this will facilitate

Although you may sometimes choose to eat cookies before they've been allowed to cool—who, after all, can resist a warm chocolate chip cookie?—always be sure to cool cookies completely before storing them.

When measuring sticky ingredients such as honey and peanut butter, always grease the measuring cup first, as this will make removal easier.

When measuring butter, remember that a 1/4-pound stick equals 1/2 cup, or 8 tablespoons. Usually, the butter wrapper has table- spoons clearly marked, making it easy to measure out the proper amount.

easy removal. A rubber spatula will further aid you in scraping every last bit out of the cup.

❏ When measuring butter, soften the butter only until it is malleable enough to be packed into a dry measuring cup. Then level off the top with a straight edge.

❏ Measure brown sugar by packing it firmly into a dry measuring cup and leveling it off with a straight edge. When the sugar is turned out of the cup, it should hold its shape.

❏ When measuring raisins and other soft, chunky ingredients, press them into the measuring cup. When measuring dry, chunky ingre- dients—chocolate chips and chopped nuts, for instance—spoon the ingredient into the cup, tap the cup against the table to make the ingredients settle, and add more if necessary.

Mixing the Dough

Nearly every Mason jar cookie recipe requires that you cream the but- ter with one or more of the other ingredients, such as the vanilla extract or the egg. This is the most important step in cookie mixing as it helps insure the proper blending of the cookie dough ingredients and also incorporates air into the batter, which will enable your baking soda and baking powder do their work. Although I use a portable mixer to cream the required ingredients, this step can also be performed with a wooden spoon or a fork. Just keep mixing or beating until the ingre- dients are well blended and the mixture is light in color and fluffy in consistency.

If the butter becomes runny, rather than light and fluffy, while you're creaming it, simply place the bowl in the refrigerator until the mixture becomes firm. Then begin creaming it again.

Once the butter has been creamed, most recipes will direct you to add the dry ingredients to the butter. In some cases, the ingredients can be combined with either a wooden spoon *or* an electric mixer set on low speed. Be aware, though, that when the ingredients include chocolate chips or other goodies that might be chopped up by an electric mixer, it's best to use a spoon. Whichever tool you use, do not overmix the dough, but beat or stir only until the ingredients are combined.

Forming and Baking the Cookies

The vast majority of Mason jar cookies are drop cookies, meaning that you form the cookies by scooping the dough up with a teaspoon and dropping it onto the baking sheet. Cookie doughs vary in consistency. Some will fall easily from the spoon, and some may need a push from a second spoon. To make the cookies uniform in size, use a measuring teaspoon rather than the teaspoon from your everyday flatware, and scoop up a heaping teaspoonful.

When a recipe directs you to form the dough into balls, make sure that the dough is stiff enough to handle easily. If not, chill the dough until it reaches the proper consistency and, if necessary, lightly dust your hands with a little flour or powdered sugar to prevent the dough from sticking. With a little practice, you'll soon be able to form balls of a consistent size.

Cookie dough must also be relatively stiff when the recipe directs you to roll and cut it. If the dough seems soft and sticky, refrigerate it for twenty minutes or so. Then *lightly* dust the work surface with a little flour, and use a rolling pin to form the dough into a sheet of the correct thickness. If sticking continues to be a problem, you can also dust

Although electric mixers can sometimes be used to blend wet and dry ingredients, whenever a cookie dough contains chocolate chips or other chunky ingredients that you want to remain whole, you'll enjoy best results by mixing with a wooden spoon.

When forming cookie dough into balls, first dust your hands with flour or powdered sugar to prevent sticking. If the dough is dark, dust your hands with cocoa powder instead.

Baking times vary from oven to oven, and can even differ because of variations in ingredients. For best results, check cookies for doneness at the minimum baking time.

the rolling pin with a little flour. Don't use too much flour, though, as an excessive amount of flour will create a tough cookie. After cutting the dough, place the remaining pieces in the refrigerator so that they will again become firm enough to roll and cut.

As the cookies are formed, place them at least two inches apart on your cookie sheet, as this will allow for spreading. It is not necessary to grease the baking sheet unless the recipe specifically directs you to do so.

Bake only one sheet of cookies at a time, and make sure that the sheet is on the middle rack of the oven with at least one inch between the edge of the pan and the oven itself. This will promote proper air flow and even heating.

Most ovens run either a little hotter or a little cooler than the temperature to which they're set, so be aware that you may have to compensate by adjusting either the temperature to which the oven is set or the baking time. (I recommend using an oven thermometer to determine the precise temperature.) Since baking time and oven temperature affect the cookie's final texture, you may also choose to make adjustments according to your personal preferences. If you want your cookies to be chewy, slightly underbake them. If you want them to be crisp, bake them a little longer. In most cases, cookies are done when they are slightly browned around the edges. A watchful eye is very important when baking cookies, as they can quickly turn from *done* to *hard*.

Allow your Mason jar cookies to cool for about 5 minutes before removing them from the baking sheet. Then transfer them to a wire rack to cool completely. Never leave them on the hot baking sheet, or they'll continue to cook.

When your cookies are ready to be removed from the oven, place the baking sheet on a heatproof surface for five minutes to allow the cookies to cool slightly. Then use a spatula to transfer the cookies to a rack or plate, and cool completely before serving or storing in an airtight container.

CREATING THE JARS

Although you'll want to bake and enjoy Mason jar cookies often, you'll also take pleasure in giving Mason jar cookie mixes to friends and family. These mixes make perfect gifts during the holidays, on birthdays, or just as thoughtful thank-yous.

Fortunately, Mason jar cookie mixes are easy—and fun—to create. Below, you'll learn about the few simple materials you'll need to get started, and you'll discover how to use them to craft beautiful mixes that are a joy to give and receive.

Choosing the Materials

The materials needed to make Mason jar cookie mixes are inexpensive and few in number. Keep these items on hand, and you'll be able to create a gift at a moment's notice.

The Jar

For each cookie mix you make, you will need a clean, dry, one-quart wide-mouth Mason jar with a screw-on top. While other containers may also be suitable, the large opening of a Mason jar will give you the room you need to pour in the ingredients, tamp them down firmly into even layers, and periodically wipe the inside of the jar with a dry paper towel during filling so that the final gift has a neat, clean appearance.

Cookie mixes can be packed in a variety of jars, but the wide mouth of a Mason-type jar makes it easy to create neat, attractive layers of ingredients.

The Fabric and Tie

When you finish filling your Mason jar, the appealing layers of ingredients—brown sugar, raisins, and chocolate chips, for instance—will

When looking for fabrics to trim the top of your Mason jar mix, be sure to check the remnants pile at your local fabric or crafts store. Often, you'll be able to decorate a number of gifts for just a few dollars.

instantly turn the container into an attractive gift. Many people, in fact, use the unadorned jars to decorate their kitchens and pantries! But you can further enhance the charm of the mix by tying a square of decorative fabric to the top.

For each jar, you will need a seven-by-seven-inch piece of fabric, cut with either regular fabric scissors or pinking shears. When choosing your fabric, be creative. A square of denim, burlap, or calico would create a delightful country look, for instance, while a red-and-green fabric would be the perfect finishing touch for a Christmas gift. Often, fabric stores offer inexpensive remnants, each of which could adorn several jars.

Be sure to select a tie that complements your fabric. A length of sisal twine or yarn would make an appropriate tie for your calico square, for example, while a slender gold or silver ribbon would beautifully complete your holiday gift. Just make sure that you buy a long enough tie for each piece. A forty-eight-inch length will allow you to securely attach the fabric, as well as your tag, to the jar.

The Tag

Your tag will provide the all-important information that the recipient of the jar will need to turn the cookie mix into a batch of homemade treats. Each tag should supply the name of the cookie recipe, the yield of the recipe, the list of ingredients that must be added to the mix (eggs and butter, for instance), and the baking instructions themselves.

Make sure that your gift tag includes the name of the cookie recipe, the yield of the recipe, the list of ingredients that must be added to the mix, and the baking instructions.

Feel free to make a no-fuss tag or to craft one that showcases your creativity and flair. The right-hand page of each recipe contains a boxed copy of the tag information for those cookies. If you like, you can simply make a photocopy of this box, using the paper of your choice; cut the photocopy out with plain scissors or pinking shears; and attach the printed tag to your jar with the selected tie. Or you may choose to cut out a piece of sturdy paper—a three-by-four-inch size is usually adequate—and write out the instructions in your own clear handwriting or in calligraphy. If you have a computer, of course, your options are even greater. Consider typing in the instructions and printing them out in a beautiful (but readable) font. Add a decorative border, if you wish. You can even print the instructions directly onto stickers and affix a sticker to each jar in place of a tag. The possibilities are endless.

Packing the Ingredients

Believe it or not, the order in which the ingredients are packed in your Mason jar can make a *big* difference. Imagine, for instance, pouring the granulated sugar over a layer of chocolate chips. Gradually, the sugar will sift between the chips, mixing the layers and creating a messy appearance. That's why the white sugar is so often placed over a layer of brown sugar or oatmeal.

By following the order of ingredients prescribed on the right-hand page of each two-page recipe spread, you will be sure to create an attractive jar. Be aware, though, that in most cases, this isn't the *only* way in which the ingredients can be successfully layered. I have usually chosen to provide you with the simplest method of packing the jar. If you prefer, you can break some of the ingredients into two parts and create your own custom jar of contrasting layers. If you turn to page 93, you'll see what I mean. In the diagram for Rainbow Kids Cookies, the oatmeal and brown sugar have each been divided into two layers

Tag making can be as simple or as creative as you like. For a fuss-free tag, just photocopy the boxed instructions provided in the recipe. Other options include writing the directions out in calligraphy and generating tags or labels on your home computer.

for maximum effect. After you make a few gift jars and you get a feel for the process, you may want to customize your jars using this technique. To keep your layers as neat as possible, just remember to avoid placing powdery or granular ingredients—flour and sugar, for instance—above a product such as chocolate chips, nuts, or raisins. Because chips and the like have space between the individual pieces, they will allow the powdery substance to sift in. Instead, try to pack an ingredient such as brown sugar above these goodies, as the moist sugar will form a "seal" below the powder, preventing the layers from blending together.

As you create your Mason jar mixes, be sure to pack the ingredients firmly. After pouring in each ingredient, use a long-handled tart tamper; the squeezable bulb section of a turkey baster; or the bottom of a long, slim glass to press the addition into an even layer. Then, before adding the next ingredient, wipe the inside of the jar with a dry paper towel to achieve a clean, professional appearance.

> Once completed, your Mason jar cookie mix should be stored in a cool, dry place, where it will remain fresh for up to twelve months.

After all the layers of the cookie mix have been added, simply screw on the top of the jar, tightening it as much as possible to keep the mix fresh. Now you're ready to complete the gift.

Decorating the Jar

To add the finishing touches to your jarred mix, simply center the chosen fabric square on the lid of the jar and secure it with a rubber band. Then wrap your chosen tie around the rubber band twice, covering the band, and knot the tie to hold it in place.

Using a hole punch, make a hole in the tag and slide the tie through the hole, threading it through once or twice and tying it off with a bow.

If you've chosen to photocopy the boxed tag provided on the right-hand page of each recipe, you may want to fold the left side of the tag over the right before punching a hole in the top left-hand corner. This will allow you to thread the tie through two layers of paper, attaching your tag securely to the jar.

Finally, to make your Mason jar cookie mix even more special, you may want to use the same ribbon or twine to attach a wooden spoon or, if the cookies are to be rolled and cut, a cookie cutter. Your Mason jar cookie mix is now done, ready for its lucky recipient!

HOW TO USE THIS BOOK

The Mason Jar Cookie Cookbook has a unique format that allows you to easily bake cookies in your kitchen or create a beautiful Mason jar cookie mix.

First, use the table of contents or the index to choose a recipe that suits your fancy. You will find that the directions for each recipe fall on two facing pages. On the left-hand page, you'll find instructions for baking the cookies at home. On the right-hand page, you'll find instructions for creating a Mason jar cookie mix.

If you have decided to bake a pan of cookies, simply look at the left-hand page of the two-page recipe spread. You'll see that the ingredients have been broken into two lists. The first list—the Jar Ingredients—contains the nonperishable ingredients that would be placed in the jar if you were creating a mix. These items have been grouped together here for ease of mixing, as in most cases, all the Jar Ingredients get combined first. The second list presents the Additional Ingredients—the eggs, butter, and other items that must be added to the mix to create the

By following the diagram included in each recipe, you'll be sure to create an attractive Mason jar mix. Just remember to place the ingredient shown at the bottom of the diagram in the jar first.

cookie dough. The numbered instructions will tell you exactly how to use your ingredients to bake delicious cookies each and every time.

If your goal is to craft a cookie mix gift, look at the right-hand page. The numbered material at the top of the page outlines the steps for creating the jar. (For more details, see pages 19 to 23 of this chapter.) Next to these instructions, you'll find a diagram that shows you how to fill the jar for attractive results. (Just remember that the layer shown at the *bottom* of the diagram should be placed in the jar *first*.) Finally, at the bottom of the page, you'll find all the information you need for your tag. As discussed on pages 20 to 21, you can photocopy the tag directly from the book and attach the copy to your jar, or, if you prefer, you can write these instructions out on decorative paper.

Cookie baking is a wonderfully satisfying experience. With very little fuss or bother, you can produce delightful confections that are sure to bring smiles to the faces of friends and family alike. And with the *The Mason Jar Cookie Cookbook,* you can also give the gift of home baking to everyone on your gift list. However you choose to use this book, I'm sure it will bring pleasing results and a satisfied sweet tooth. Enjoy!

CookieRecipes

APPLESAUCECOOKIES

These light cookies are very much like apple cake—only crisper.

YIELD:
3 DOZEN COOKIES

JAR INGREDIENTS

2 ¼ cups all-purpose
flour

I cup brown sugar

¾ cup dark raisins

¾ cup chopped
walnuts

¾ teaspoon ground
cinnamon

½ teaspoon baking
soda

½ teaspoon salt

ADDITIONAL
INGREDIENTS

¾ cup butter,
softened

I egg

½ cup applesauce

1. Preheat the oven to 350°F.

2. Place all of the jar ingredients in a medium-sized bowl, and stir until well combined. Set aside.

3. Place the butter, egg, and applesauce in a large bowl, and cream with an electric mixer set on low speed or with a fork.

4. Add the dry ingredients to the butter mixture, and blend with a mixer set on low speed or with a spoon until well combined.

5. Drop the dough by heaping teaspoonfuls onto an ungreased baking sheet, spacing the cookies about 2 inches apart to allow for spreading.

6. Bake for 9 to 11 minutes, or until light brown in color. Allow to cool for 5 minutes on the baking sheet. Then transfer to wire racks and cool completely.

7. Serve immediately, or store in an airtight container for up to 2 weeks.

CREATINGTHEJAR

¾ cup chopped walnuts

¾ cup dark raisins

¾ teaspoon ground cinnamon

½ teaspoon salt

½ teaspoon baking soda

2¼ cups all-purpose flour

1 cup brown sugar

1. Wash and thoroughly dry a 1-quart wide-mouth canning jar.

2. Layer the ingredients in the jar as shown at left, pressing firmly with a flat-bottomed object, such as a tart tamper or the bottom of a narrow glass, after each addition. Make the layers as level as possible.

3. Secure the lid, and decorate as desired. (See page 22.) Attach the instructions for making the cookies found below.

Yield:
3 dozen cookies

In addition to the contents of the jar, you will need to add the following ingredients:

¾ cup butter, softened

1 egg

½ cup applesauce

APPLESAUCE COOKIES

Preheat the oven to 350°F. In a large bowl, cream the butter, egg, and applesauce. Add the contents of the jar, and stir until well mixed. Drop the dough by heaping teaspoonfuls onto an ungreased baking sheet, spacing the cookies about 2 inches apart. Bake for 9 to 11 minutes, or until light brown in color. Allow to cool for 5 minutes on the baking sheet. Then transfer to wire racks and cool completely. Serve immediately, or store in an airtight container for up to 2 weeks.

BESTEVER**CHOCOLATE** **CHIP**COOKIES

The warm kitchen will entice you with the aroma of these chocolate chip
cookies before you even take the first luscious bite.

YIELD:
2 1/2 DOZEN COOKIES

JAR INGREDIENTS

1 2/3 cups all-purpose
flour

1 1/2 cups semisweet
chocolate chips

1/2 cup sugar

1/2 cup brown sugar

3/4 teaspoon baking
soda

ADDITIONAL
INGREDIENTS

1/2 cup butter,
softened

2 eggs

1 teaspoon vanilla
extract

1. Preheat the oven to 375°F.

2. Place all of the jar ingredients in a medium-sized bowl, and stir until well combined. Set aside.

3. Place the butter, eggs, and vanilla extract in a large bowl, and cream with an electric mixer set on low speed or with a fork.

4. Add the dry ingredients to the butter mixture, and mix with a spoon until well combined.

5. Drop the dough by heaping teaspoonfuls onto an ungreased baking sheet, spacing the cookies about 2 inches apart to allow for spreading.

6. Bake for 8 to 10 minutes, or until light brown in color. Allow to cool for 5 minutes on the baking sheet. Then transfer to wire racks and cool completely.

7. Serve immediately, or store in an airtight container for up to 2 weeks.

CREATING THE JAR

1½ cups semisweet
chocolate chips

½ cup brown sugar

½ cup sugar

¾ teaspoon baking soda

1⅔ cups all-purpose flour

1. Wash and thoroughly dry a 1-quart wide-mouth canning jar.

2. Layer the ingredients in the jar as shown at left, pressing firmly with a flat-bottomed object, such as a tart tamper or the bottom of a narrow glass, after each addition. Make the layers as level as possible.

3. Secure the lid, and decorate as desired. (See page 22.) Attach the instructions for making the cookies found below.

Yield:
2½ dozen cookies

In addition to the contents
of the jar, you will need to add
the following ingredients:

½ cup butter, softened

2 eggs

1 teaspoon vanilla extract

BEST EVER CHOCOLATE CHIP COOKIES

Preheat the oven to 375°F. In a large bowl, cream the butter, eggs, and vanilla extract. Add the contents of the jar, and stir until well mixed. Drop the dough by heaping teaspoonfuls onto an ungreased baking sheet, spacing the cookies about 2 inches apart. Bake for 8 to 10 minutes, or until light brown in color. Allow to cool for 5 minutes on the baking sheet. Then transfer to wire racks and cool completely. Serve immediately, or store in an airtight container for up to 2 weeks.

BROWNAND**WHITE**CRISPIES

YIELD:
3 DOZEN COOKIES

This combination of white and dark chocolate chips, oatmeal,
and crisped rice cereal is sure to please any cookie lover!

JAR INGREDIENTS

1 ½ cups all-purpose
flour

½ cup brown sugar

½ cup sugar

½ cup quick-cooking
oatmeal

½ cup crisped rice
cereal

½ cup white
chocolate chips

½ cup semisweet
chocolate chips

¾ teaspoon baking
soda

¼ teaspoon baking
powder

ADDITIONAL
INGREDIENTS

½ cup butter,
softened

1 egg

2 tablespoons water

1. Preheat the oven to 350°F.

2. Place all of the jar ingredients in a medium-sized bowl, and stir until well combined. Set aside.

3. Place the butter, egg, and water in a large bowl, and cream with an electric mixer set on low speed or with a fork.

4. Add the dry ingredients to the butter mixture, and mix with a spoon until well combined.

5. Drop the dough by heaping teaspoonfuls onto an ungreased baking sheet, spacing the cookies about 2 inches apart to allow for spreading.

6. Bake for 10 to 12 minutes, or until light brown in color. Allow to cool for 5 minutes on the baking sheet. Then transfer to wire racks and cool completely.

7. Serve immediately, or store in an airtight container for up to 2 weeks.

CREATINGTHEJAR

½ cup sugar

½ cup quick-cooking oatmeal

½ cup semisweet chocolate chips

½ cup brown sugar

½ cup white chocolate chips

½ cup crisped rice cereal

¼ teaspoon baking powder

¾ teaspoon baking soda

1 ½ cups all-purpose flour

1. Wash and thoroughly dry a 1-quart wide-mouth canning jar.

2. Layer the ingredients in the jar as shown at left, pressing firmly with a flat-bottomed object, such as a tart tamper or the bottom of a narrow glass, after each addition. Make the layers as level as possible.

3. Secure the lid, and decorate as desired. (See page 22.) Attach the instructions for making the cookies found below.

Yield: 3 dozen cookies

In addition to the contents of the jar, you will need to add the following ingredients:

½ cup butter, softened

1 egg

2 tablespoons water

Brown and White Crispies

Preheat the oven to 350°F. In a large bowl, cream the butter, egg, and water. Add the contents of the jar, and stir until well mixed. Drop the dough by heaping teaspoonfuls onto an ungreased baking sheet, spacing the cookies about 2 inches apart. Bake for 10 to 12 minutes, or until light brown in color. Allow to cool for 5 minutes on the baking sheet. Then transfer to wire racks and cool completely. Serve immediately, or store in an airtight container for up to 2 weeks.

BROWNSUGAR**NUT**COOKIES

Simple ingredients are the secret behind these delicious cookies.
If you like, make the dough in advance and store in the
refrigerator for up to three days before baking.

YIELD:
2¹/₂ DOZEN COOKIES

JAR INGREDIENTS

1³/₄ cups all-purpose
flour

1¹/₄ cups chopped
walnuts

1 cup brown sugar

1 teaspoon baking
soda

¹/₂ teaspoon salt

**ADDITIONAL
INGREDIENTS**

¹/₂ cup butter,
softened

1 egg

1 teaspoon vanilla
extract

1. Preheat the oven to 350°F.

2. Place all of the jar ingredients in a medium-sized bowl, and stir until well combined. Set aside.

3. Place the butter, egg, and vanilla extract in a large bowl, and cream with an electric mixer set on low speed or with a fork.

4. Add the dry ingredients to the butter mixture, and blend with a mixer set on low speed or with a spoon until well combined.

5. Drop the dough by heaping teaspoonfuls onto an ungreased baking sheet, spacing the cookies about 2 inches apart to allow for spreading.

6. Bake for 10 to 12 minutes, or until light brown in color. Allow to cool for 5 minutes on the baking sheet. Then transfer to wire racks and cool completely.

7. Serve immediately, or store in an airtight container for up to 2 weeks.

CREATING THE JAR

1 ¼ cups chopped walnuts

½ teaspoon salt

1 teaspoon baking soda

1 ¾ cups all-purpose flour

1 cup brown sugar

1. Wash and thoroughly dry a 1-quart wide-mouth canning jar.

2. Layer the ingredients in the jar as shown at left, pressing firmly with a flat-bottomed object, such as a tart tamper or the bottom of a narrow glass, after each addition. Make the layers as level as possible.

3. Secure the lid, and decorate as desired. (See page 22.) Attach the instructions for making the cookies found below.

Yield:
2 ½ dozen cookies

In addition to the contents of the jar, you will need to add the following ingredients:

½ cup butter, softened

1 egg

1 teaspoon vanilla extract

BROWN SUGAR NUT COOKIES

Preheat the oven to 350°F. In a large bowl, cream the butter, egg, and vanilla extract. Add the contents of the jar, and stir until well mixed. Drop the dough by heaping teaspoonfuls onto an ungreased baking sheet, spacing the cookies about 2 inches apart. Bake for 10 to 12 minutes, or until light brown in color. Allow to cool for 5 minutes on the baking sheet. Then transfer to wire racks and cool completely. Serve immediately, or store in an airtight container for up to 2 weeks.

BUTTERSCOTCHCHIP COOKIES

YIELD:
3 DOZEN COOKIES

JAR INGREDIENTS

1 1/8 cups all-purpose
flour

1 cup sweetened
flaked coconut

1/2 cup crisped rice
cereal

3/4 cup butterscotch
chips

1/2 cup chopped
pecans

1/2 cup brown sugar

1/2 cup sugar

1/2 teaspoon baking
soda

1/4 teaspoon baking
powder

1/4 teaspoon salt

**ADDITIONAL
INGREDIENTS**

1/2 cup butter, softened

1 egg

1/2 teaspoon vanilla
extract

*These cookies provide both buttery richness
and a delightful crunch in one easy-to-make treat.*

1. Preheat the oven to 350°F.

2. Place all of the jar ingredients in a medium-sized mixing bowl, and stir until well combined. Set aside.

3. Place the butter, egg, and vanilla extract in a large bowl, and cream with an electric mixer set on low speed or with a fork.

4. Add the dry ingredients to the butter mixture, and mix with a spoon until well combined.

5. Drop the dough by heaping teaspoonfuls onto an ungreased baking sheet, spacing the cookies about 2 inches apart to allow for spreading.

6. Bake for 9 to 12 minutes, or until light brown in color. Allow to cool for 5 minutes on the baking sheet. Then transfer to wire racks and cool completely.

7. Serve immediately, or store in an airtight container for up to 2 weeks.

CREATING THE JAR

½ cup chopped pecans

¾ cup butterscotch chips

½ cup crisped rice cereal

½ cup sugar

1 cup sweetened flaked coconut

¼ teaspoon salt

½ cup brown sugar

¼ teaspoon baking powder

½ teaspoon baking soda

1⅛ cups all-purpose flour

1. Wash and thoroughly dry a 1-quart wide-mouth canning jar.

2. Layer the ingredients in the jar as shown at left, pressing firmly with a flat-bottomed object, such as a tart tamper or the bottom of a narrow glass, after each addition. Make the layers as level as possible.

3. Secure the lid, and decorate as desired. (See page 22.) Attach the instructions for making the cookies found below.

Yield:
3 dozen cookies

In addition to the contents of the jar, you will need to add the following ingredients:

½ cup butter, softened

1 egg

½ teaspoon vanilla extract

BUTTERSCOTCH CHIP COOKIES

Preheat the oven to 350°F. In a large bowl, cream the butter, egg, and vanilla extract. Add the contents of the jar, and stir until well mixed. Drop the dough by heaping teaspoonfuls onto an ungreased baking sheet, spacing the cookies about 2 inches apart. Bake for 9 to 12 minutes, or until light brown in color. Allow to cool for 5 minutes on the baking sheet. Then transfer to wire racks and cool completely. Serve immediately, or store in an airtight container for up to 2 weeks.

CHOCOLATECHEWBACCAS

My son named these cookies after taking the first scrumptious, chewy bite.

YIELD:
3 DOZEN COOKIES

JAR INGREDIENTS

I cup milk chocolate
chips

2 cups all-purpose
flour

$^1/_2$ cup brown sugar

$^1/_2$ cup sugar

$^1/_2$ teaspoon baking
soda

$^1/_2$ teaspoon baking
powder

**ADDITIONAL
INGREDIENTS**

$^1/_2$ cup butter,
softened

2 eggs

$^1/_2$ teaspoon vanilla
extract

1. Preheat the oven to 350°F.

2. Place the chocolate chips in a microwave-safe bowl, and microwave on high power for 20 to 30 seconds, or until melted. Alternatively, place the chips in a double boiler and melt over medium heat, stirring occasionally. Set aside.

3. Place all of the remaining jar ingredients in a medium-sized bowl, and stir until well combined. Set aside.

4. Place the butter, eggs, and vanilla extract in a large bowl, and cream with an electric mixer set on low speed or with a fork.

5. Add the dry ingredients to the butter mixture, and blend with a mixer set on low speed or with a spoon until well combined.

6. Stir in the melted chocolate and mix thoroughly.

7. Drop the dough by heaping teaspoonfuls onto an ungreased baking sheet, spacing the cookies about 2 inches apart to allow for spreading.

8. Bake for 12 to 14 minutes, or until light brown in color. Allow to cool for 5 minutes on the baking sheet. Then transfer to wire racks and cool completely.

9. Serve immediately, or store in an airtight container for up to 2 weeks.

CREATING THE JAR

I cup milk chocolate
chips

¹/₂ cup sugar

¹/₂ cup brown sugar

¹/₂ teaspoon baking powder

¹/₂ teaspoon baking soda

2 cups all-purpose flour

1. Wash and thoroughly dry a 1-quart wide-mouth canning jar.

2. Layer the ingredients in the jar as shown at left, pressing firmly with a flat-bottomed object, such as a tart tamper or the bottom of a narrow glass, after each addition. Make the layers as level as possible.

3. Secure the lid, and decorate as desired. (See page 22.) Attach the instructions for making the cookies found below.

Yield:
3 dozen cookies

In addition to the contents of the jar, you will need to add the following ingredients:

¹/₂ cup butter, softened

2 eggs

¹/₂ teaspoon vanilla extract

CHOCOLATE CHEWBACCAS
Preheat the oven to 350°F. Remove the chocolate chips from the jar. Melt the chips in a microwave oven for 20 to 30 seconds, or melt in a double boiler over medium heat, and set aside. In a large bowl, cream the butter, eggs, and vanilla extract. Add the contents of the jar, and stir until well mixed. Stir in the melted chocolate chips, mixing well. Drop the dough by heaping teaspoonfuls onto an ungreased baking sheet, spacing the cookies about 2 inches apart. Bake for 12 to 14 minutes, or until light brown in color. Allow to cool for 5 minutes on the baking sheet. Then transfer to wire racks and cool completely. Serve immediately, or store in an airtight container for up to 2 weeks.

CHOCOLATE-COVERED **RAISIN**COOKIES

These chewy cookies are big on taste.
For a real treat, serve with a glass of ice-cold milk.

YIELD:
3 DOZEN COOKIES

JAR INGREDIENTS

1¾ cups all-purpose flour

1 cup chocolate-covered raisins

¾ cup sugar

½ cup milk chocolate chips

½ cup brown sugar

1 teaspoon baking powder

½ teaspoon baking soda

ADDITIONAL INGREDIENTS

½ cup butter, softened

1 egg

1 teaspoon vanilla extract

1. Preheat the oven to 375°F.

2. Place all of the jar ingredients in a medium-sized bowl, and stir until well combined. Set aside.

3. Place the butter, egg, and vanilla extract in a large bowl, and cream with an electric mixer set on low speed or with a fork.

4. Add the dry ingredients to the butter mixture, and mix with a spoon until well combined.

5. Drop the dough by heaping teaspoonfuls onto an ungreased baking sheet, spacing the cookies about 2 inches apart to allow for spreading.

6. Bake for 10 to 12 minutes, or until light brown in color. Allow to cool for 5 minutes on the baking sheet. Then transfer to wire racks and cool completely.

7. Serve immediately, or store in an airtight container for up to 2 weeks.

CREATINGTHEJAR

½ cup milk chocolate chips

1 cup chocolate-covered raisins

½ cup brown sugar

¾ cup sugar

1 teaspoon baking powder

½ teaspoon baking soda

1¾ cups all-purpose flour

1. Wash and thoroughly dry a 1-quart wide-mouth canning jar.

2. Layer the ingredients in the jar as shown at left, pressing firmly with a flat-bottomed object, such as a tart tamper or the bottom of a narrow glass, after each addition. Make the layers as level as possible.

3. Secure the lid, and decorate as desired. (See page 22.) Attach the instructions for making the cookies found below.

Yield:
3 dozen cookies

In addition to the contents of the jar, you will need to add the following ingredients:

½ cup butter, softened

1 egg

1 teaspoon vanilla extract

Chocolate-Covered Raisin Cookies

Preheat the oven to 375°F. In a large bowl, cream the butter, egg, and vanilla extract. Add the contents of the jar, and stir until well mixed. Drop the dough by heaping teaspoonfuls onto an ungreased baking sheet, spacing the cookies about 2 inches apart. Bake for 10 to 12 minutes, or until light brown in color. Allow to cool for 5 minutes on the baking sheet. Then transfer to wire racks and cool completely. Serve immediately, or store in an airtight container for up to 2 weeks.

COCONUTRAISINCOOKIES

If you love the rich flavor and satisfying chewiness of coconut,
this is the cookie for you.

YIELD:
2 1/2 DOZEN COOKIES

JAR INGREDIENTS

1 1/4 cups all-purpose
flour

1 1/4 cups sweetened
flaked coconut

3/4 cup brown sugar

1/2 cup sugar

1/2 cup quick-cooking
oatmeal

1/2 cup dark raisins

1 teaspoon baking
soda

1 teaspoon baking
powder

**ADDITIONAL
INGREDIENTS**

1/2 cup butter,
softened

1 egg

1 teaspoon vanilla
extract

1. Preheat the oven to 350°F.

2. Place all of the jar ingredients in a medium-sized bowl, and stir until well combined. Set aside.

3. Place the egg, butter, and vanilla extract in a large bowl, and cream with an electric mixer set on low speed or with a fork.

4. Add the dry ingredients to the butter mixture, and blend with a mixer set on low speed or with a spoon until well combined.

5. Drop the dough by heaping teaspoonfuls onto an ungreased baking sheet, spacing the cookies about 2 inches apart to allow for spreading.

6. Bake for 8 to 10 minutes, or until light brown in color. Allow to cool for 5 minutes on the baking sheet. Then transfer to wire racks and cool completely.

7. Serve immediately, or store in an airtight container for up to 2 weeks.

CREATING THE JAR

1/2 cup dark raisins

1 1/4 cups sweetened flaked coconut

1/2 cup sugar

3/4 cup brown sugar

1/2 cup quick-cooking oatmeal

1 teaspoon baking soda

1 teaspoon baking powder

1 1/4 cups all-purpose flour

1. Wash and thoroughly dry a 1-quart wide-mouth canning jar.

2. Layer the ingredients in the jar as shown at left, pressing firmly with a flat-bottomed object, such as a tart tamper or the bottom of a narrow glass, after each addition. Make the layers as level as possible.

3. Secure the lid, and decorate as desired. (See page 22.) Attach the instructions for making the cookies found below.

Yield: 2 1/2 dozen cookies

In addition to the contents of the jar, you will need to add the following ingredients:

1/2 cup butter, softened

1 egg

1 teaspoon vanilla extract

COCONUT RAISIN COOKIES

Preheat the oven to 350°F. In a large bowl, cream the butter, egg, and vanilla extract. Add the contents of the jar, and stir until well mixed. Drop the dough by heaping teaspoonfuls onto an ungreased baking sheet, spacing the cookies about 2 inches apart. Bake for 8 to 10 minutes, or until light brown in color. Allow to cool for 5 minutes on the baking sheet. Then transfer to wire racks and cool completely. Serve immediately, or store in an airtight container for up to 2 weeks.

CORNFLAKECOOKIES

If you enjoy the taste and texture of macaroons,
try this super-simple version.

YIELD:
3 DOZEN COOKIES

JAR INGREDIENTS

2 1/2 cups sweetened
flaked coconut

1 1/2 cups corn flakes

1 1/4 cups sugar

1/4 teaspoon salt

**ADDITIONAL
INGREDIENTS**

3 egg whites

1/2 teaspoon vanilla
extract

1. Preheat the oven to 325°F.

2. Place all of the jar ingredients in a medium-sized bowl, and stir until well combined. Set aside.

3. Place the egg whites and vanilla extract in a large bowl, and beat with an electric mixer set on high speed until stiff peaks form.

4. Using a spoon, gently fold the dry ingredients into the egg white mixture.

5. Drop the dough by heaping teaspoonfuls onto an ungreased baking sheet, spacing the cookies about 2 inches apart to allow for spreading.

6. Bake for 13 to 15 minutes, or until light brown in color. Immediately remove the cookies from the baking sheet and transfer to wire racks to cool completely.

7. Serve immediately, or store in an airtight container for up to 2 weeks.

CREATINGTHEJAR

1. Wash and thoroughly dry a 1-quart wide-mouth canning jar.

2. Layer the ingredients in the jar as shown at left, pressing firmly with a flat-bottomed object, such as a tart tamper or the bottom of a narrow glass, after each addition. Make the layers as level as possible.

3. Secure the lid, and decorate as desired. (See page 22.) Attach the instructions for making the cookies found below.

1 ½ cups corn flakes

2 ½ cups sweetened flaked coconut

¼ teaspoon salt

1 ¼ cups sugar

Yield:
3 dozen cookies

In addition to the contents of the jar, you will need to add the following ingredients:

3 egg whites

½ teaspoon vanilla extract

CORN FLAKE COOKIES

Preheat the oven to 325°F. In a large bowl, beat the egg whites and vanilla extract with an electric mixer until stiff peaks form. Using a spoon, gently fold the contents of the jar into the egg white mixture. Drop the dough by heaping teaspoonfuls onto an ungreased baking sheet, spacing the cookies about 2 inches apart. Bake for 13 to 15 minutes, or until light brown in color. Immediately transfer to wire racks and cool completely. Serve immediately, or store in an airtight container for up to 2 weeks.

COUNTRYCHOCOLATECHIP OATMEALCOOKIES

A combination of chocolate chips and oatmeal
gives this cookie a delightfully chewy texture.

YIELD:
3 DOZEN COOKIES

JAR INGREDIENTS

1 1/2 cups quick-cooking oatmeal

1 cup all-purpose flour

3/4 cup semisweet chocolate chips

1/2 cup sugar

1/2 cup brown sugar

3/4 teaspoon baking soda

1/2 teaspoon salt

ADDITIONAL INGREDIENTS

1/2 cup butter, softened

2 eggs

1 teaspoon vanilla extract

1. Preheat the oven to 375°F.

2. Place all of the jar ingredients in a medium-sized bowl, and stir until well combined. Set aside.

3. Place the butter, eggs, and vanilla extract in a large bowl, and cream with an electric mixer set on low speed or with a fork.

4. Add the dry ingredients to the butter mixture, and mix with a spoon until well combined.

5. Drop the dough by heaping teaspoonfuls onto an ungreased baking sheet, spacing the cookies about 2 inches apart to allow for spreading.

6. Bake for 12 to 14 minutes, or until light brown in color. Allow to cool for 5 minutes on the baking sheet. Then transfer to wire racks and cool completely.

7. Serve immediately, or store in an airtight container for up to 2 weeks.

CREATINGTHEJAR

¾ cup semisweet chocolate chips

1½ cups quick-cooking oatmeal

½ teaspoon salt

¾ teaspoon baking soda

1 cup all-purpose flour

½ cup brown sugar

½ cup sugar

1. Wash and thoroughly dry a 1-quart wide-mouth canning jar.

2. Layer the ingredients in the jar as shown at left, pressing firmly with a flat-bottomed object, such as a tart tamper or the bottom of a narrow glass, after each addition. Make the layers as level as possible.

3. Secure the lid, and decorate as desired. (See page 22.) Attach the instructions for making the cookies found below.

Yield:
3 dozen cookies

In addition to the contents of the jar, you will need to add the following ingredients:

½ cup butter, softened

2 eggs

1 teaspoon vanilla extract

COUNTRY CHOCOLATE CHIP OATMEAL COOKIES

Preheat the oven to 375°F. In a large bowl, cream the butter, eggs, and vanilla extract. Add the contents of the jar, and stir until well mixed. Drop the dough by heaping teaspoonfuls onto an ungreased baking sheet, spacing the cookies about 2 inches apart. Bake for 12 to 14 minutes, or until light brown in color. Allow to cool for 5 minutes on the baking sheet. Then transfer to wire racks and cool completely. Serve immediately, or store in an airtight container for up to 2 weeks.

COWBOYCOOKIES

Accompanied by a glass of milk, these cookies will make a great
after-school snack for your little cowboys and cowgirls.

YIELD:
3 DOZEN COOKIES

JAR INGREDIENTS

1 1/3 cups all-purpose flour

1 1/3 cups quick-cooking oatmeal

1 cup semisweet chocolate chips

1/2 cup brown sugar

1/2 cup sugar

1 teaspoon baking soda

1 teaspoon baking powder

1/4 teaspoon salt

ADDITIONAL INGREDIENTS

1/2 cup butter, softened

1 egg

1 teaspoon vanilla extract

1. Preheat the oven to 350°F.

2. Place all of the jar ingredients in a medium-sized bowl, and stir until well combined. Set aside.

3. Place the butter, egg, and vanilla extract in a large bowl, and cream with an electric mixer set on low speed or with a fork.

4. Add the dry ingredients to the butter mixture, and mix with a spoon until well combined.

5. Drop the dough by heaping teaspoonfuls onto an ungreased baking sheet, spacing the cookies about 2 inches apart to allow for spreading.

6. Bake for 11 to 13 minutes, or until light brown in color. Allow to cool for 5 minutes on the baking sheet. Then transfer to wire racks and cool completely.

7. Serve immediately, or store in an airtight container for up to 2 weeks.

CREATING THE JAR

I cup semisweet
chocolate chips

1 ⅓ cups quick-cooking oatmeal

½ cup brown sugar

½ cup sugar

I teaspoon baking soda

I teaspoon baking powder

¼ teaspoon salt

1 ⅓ cups all-purpose flour

1. Wash and thoroughly dry a 1-quart wide-mouth canning jar.

2. Layer the ingredients in the jar as shown at left, pressing firmly with a flat-bottomed object, such as a tart tamper or the bottom of a narrow glass, after each addition. Make the layers as level as possible.

3. Secure the lid, and decorate as desired. (See page 22.) Attach the instructions for making the cookies found below.

Yield:
3 dozen cookies

In addition to the contents of the jar, you will need to add the following ingredients:

½ cup butter, softened

I egg

I teaspoon vanilla extract

COWBOY COOKIES

Preheat the oven to 350°F. In a large bowl, cream the butter, egg, and vanilla extract. Add the contents of the jar, and stir until well mixed. Drop the dough by heaping teaspoonfuls onto an ungreased baking sheet, spacing the cookies about 2 inches apart. Bake for 11 to 13 minutes, or until light brown in color. Allow to cool for 5 minutes on the baking sheet. Then transfer to wire racks and cool completely. Serve immediately, or store in an airtight container for up to 2 weeks.

CRANBERRY CREAM DROPS

YIELD:
2 1/2 DOZEN COOKIES

JAR INGREDIENTS

1 1/8 cups all-purpose flour

1 cup quick-cooking oatmeal

1/2 cup dried cranberries

1/2 cup vanilla chips

1/2 cup chopped pecans

1/3 cup sugar

1/3 cup brown sugar

1/2 teaspoon salt

1/2 teaspoon baking soda

ADDITIONAL INGREDIENTS

1/2 cup butter, softened

2 eggs

1 teaspoon vanilla extract

The jarred mix for these cookies is so attractive that you'll be tempted to keep it in your pantry as a permanent display. That would be a shame, though, as these cranberry-studded treats are a true delight.

1. Preheat the oven to 350°F.

2. Place all of the jar ingredients in a medium-sized bowl, and stir until well combined. Set aside.

3. Place the butter, eggs, and vanilla extract in a large bowl, and cream with an electric mixer set on low speed or with a fork.

4. Add the dry ingredients to the butter mixture, and mix with a spoon until well combined.

5. Drop the dough by heaping teaspoonfuls onto an ungreased baking sheet, spacing the cookies about 2 inches apart to allow for spreading.

6. Bake for 12 to 15 minutes, or until light brown in color. Allow to cool for 5 minutes on the baking sheet. Then transfer to wire racks and cool completely.

7. Serve immediately, or store in an airtight container for up to 2 weeks.

CREATINGTHEJAR

½ cup chopped pecans

½ cup vanilla chips

½ cup dried cranberries

1 cup quick-cooking oatmeal

⅓ cup brown sugar

⅓ cup sugar

½ teaspoon salt

½ teaspoon baking soda

1⅛ cups all-purpose flour

1. Wash and thoroughly dry a 1-quart wide-mouth canning jar.

2. Layer the ingredients in the jar as shown at left, pressing firmly with a flat-bottomed object, such as a tart tamper or the bottom of a narrow glass, after each addition. Make the layers as level as possible.

3. Secure the lid, and decorate as desired. (See page 22.) Attach the instructions for making the cookies found below.

Yield:
2½ dozen cookies

In addition to the contents of the jar, you will need to add the following ingredients:

½ cup butter, softened

2 eggs

1 teaspoon vanilla extract

CRANBERRY CREAM DROPS

Preheat the oven to 350°F. In a large bowl, cream the butter, eggs, and vanilla extract. Add the contents of the jar, and stir until well mixed. Drop the dough by heaping teaspoonfuls onto an ungreased baking sheet, spacing the cookies about 2 inches apart. Bake for 12 to 15 minutes, or until light brown in color. Allow to cool for 5 minutes on the baking sheet. Then transfer to wire racks and cool completely. Serve immediately, or store in an airtight container for up to 2 weeks.

CRUNCHYCHUNKYCOOKIES

Combining the crunch of corn flakes with the richness of chocolate chips, these satisfying cookies make a wonderful lunch-box treat!

YIELD:
2 1/2 DOZEN COOKIES

JAR INGREDIENTS

1 cup all-purpose flour

1 cup quick-cooking oatmeal

3/4 cup crushed corn flakes

3/4 cup semisweet chocolate chips

3/4 cup brown sugar

1/2 cup sugar

2 tablespoons sweetened flaked coconut

3/4 teaspoon baking soda

1/2 teaspoon baking powder

1/4 teaspoon salt

ADDITIONAL INGREDIENTS

1/2 cup butter, softened

1 egg

1/4 teaspoon vanilla extract

1. Preheat the oven to 350°F.

2. Place all of the jar ingredients in a medium-sized bowl, and stir until well combined. Set aside.

3. Place the butter, egg, and vanilla extract in a large bowl, and cream with an electric mixer set on low speed or with a fork.

4. Add the dry ingredients to the butter mixture, and mix with a spoon until well combined.

5. Drop the dough by heaping teaspoonfuls onto an ungreased baking sheet, spacing the cookies about 2 inches apart to allow for spreading.

6. Bake for 10 to 12 minutes, or until light brown in color. Allow to cool for 5 minutes on the baking sheet. Then transfer to wire racks and cool completely.

7. Serve immediately, or store in an airtight container for up to 2 weeks.

CREATINGTHEJAR

1 cup quick-cooking
oatmeal

2 tablespoons sweetened
flaked coconut

¾ cup semisweet chocolate chips

¾ cup crushed corn flakes

¾ cup brown sugar

½ cup sugar

¼ teaspoon salt

¾ teaspoon baking soda

½ teaspoon baking powder

1 cup all-purpose flour

1. Wash and thoroughly dry a 1-quart wide-mouth canning jar.

2. Layer the ingredients in the jar as shown at left, pressing firmly with a flat-bottomed object, such as a tart tamper or the bottom of a narrow glass, after each addition. Make the layers as level as possible.

3. Secure the lid, and decorate as desired. (See page 22.) Attach the instructions for making the cookies found below.

Yield:
2½ dozen cookies

In addition to the contents of the jar, you will need to add the following ingredients:

½ cup butter, softened

1 egg

¼ teaspoon vanilla extract

CRUNCHY CHUNKY COOKIES

Preheat the oven to 350°F. In a large bowl, cream the butter, egg, and vanilla extract. Add the contents of the jar, and stir until well mixed. Drop the dough by heaping teaspoonfuls onto an ungreased baking sheet, spacing the cookies about 2 inches apart. Bake for 10 to 12 minutes, or until light brown in color. Allow to cool for 5 minutes on the baking sheet. Then transfer to wire racks and cool completely. Serve immediately, or store in an airtight container for up to 2 weeks.

DEATH BY CHOCOLATE COOKIES

A luscious marriage of chocolate cake and chocolate chips makes this cookie a wise choice for the chocoholic in your life.

YIELD:
3 DOZEN COOKIES

JAR INGREDIENTS

2 cups all-purpose flour

1 ½ cups sugar

½ cup semisweet chocolate chips

¾ cup unsweetened cocoa powder

1 teaspoon baking soda

½ teaspoon salt

ADDITIONAL INGREDIENTS

1 ¼ cups butter, softened

2 eggs

1 teaspoon vanilla extract

1. Preheat the oven to 350°F.

2. Place all of the jar ingredients in a medium-sized bowl, and stir until well combined. Set aside.

3. Place the butter, eggs, and vanilla extract in a large bowl, and cream with an electric mixer set on low speed or with a fork.

4. Add the dry ingredients to the butter mixture, and mix with a spoon until well combined.

5. Drop the dough by heaping teaspoonfuls onto an ungreased baking sheet, spacing the cookies about 2 inches apart to allow for spreading.

6. Bake for 8 to 10 minutes, or until light brown in color. Allow to cool for 5 minutes on the baking sheet. Then transfer to wire racks and cool completely.

7. Serve immediately, or store in an airtight container for up to 2 weeks.

CREATING THE JAR

½ cup semisweet
chocolate chips

1½ cups sugar

¾ cup unsweetened
cocoa powder

½ teaspoon salt

1 teaspoon baking soda

2 cups all-purpose flour

1. Wash and thoroughly dry a 1-quart wide-mouth canning jar.

2. Layer the ingredients in the jar as shown at left, pressing firmly with a flat-bottomed object, such as a tart tamper or the bottom of a narrow glass, after each addition. Make the layers as level as possible.

3. Secure the lid, and decorate as desired. (See page 22.) Attach the instructions for making the cookies found below.

Yield:
3 dozen cookies

In addition to the contents of the jar, you will need to add the following ingredients:

1¼ cups butter, softened

2 eggs

1 teaspoon vanilla extract

DEATH BY CHOCOLATE COOKIES

Preheat the oven to 350°F. In a large bowl, cream the butter, eggs, and vanilla extract. Add the contents of the jar, and stir until well mixed. Drop the dough by heaping teaspoonfuls onto an ungreased baking sheet, spacing the cookies about 2 inches apart. Bake for 8 to 10 minutes, or until light brown in color. Allow to cool for 5 minutes on the baking sheet. Then transfer to wire racks and cool completely. Serve immediately, or store in an airtight container for up to 2 weeks.

DREAMSICLECOOKIES

The orange-flavored drink mix combined with vanilla chips
will remind you of that favorite childhood Popsicle.

YIELD:
3 DOZEN COOKIES

JAR INGREDIENTS

1 3/4 cups all-purpose
flour

1 1/2 cups vanilla chips

3/4 cup sugar

1/2 cup orange-
flavored drink mix,
such as Tang breakfast
drink

1/2 teaspoon baking
soda

1/2 teaspoon baking
powder

ADDITIONAL
INGREDIENTS

1/2 cup butter,
softened

1 egg

1 teaspoon vanilla
extract

1. Preheat the oven to 375°F.

2. Place all of the jar ingredients in a medium-sized bowl, and stir until well combined. Set aside.

3. Place the butter, egg, and vanilla extract in a large bowl, and cream with an electric mixer set on low speed or with a fork.

4. Add the dry ingredients to the butter mixture, and mix with a spoon until well combined.

5. Drop the dough by heaping teaspoonfuls onto an ungreased baking sheet, spacing the cookies about 2 inches apart to allow for spreading.

6. Bake for 8 to 10 minutes, or until light brown in color. Allow to cool for 5 minutes on the baking sheet. Then transfer to wire racks and cool completely.

7. Serve immediately, or store in an airtight container for up to 2 weeks.

CREATINGTHEJAR

1½ cups vanilla chips

½ cup orange-flavored drink mix

¾ cup sugar

½ teaspoon baking soda

½ teaspoon baking powder

1¾ cups all-purpose flour

1. Wash and thoroughly dry a 1-quart wide-mouth canning jar.

2. Layer the ingredients in the jar as shown at left, pressing firmly with a flat-bottomed object, such as a tart tamper or the bottom of a narrow glass, after each addition. Make the layers as level as possible.

3. Secure the lid, and decorate as desired. (See page 22.) Attach the instructions for making the cookies found below.

Yield:
3 dozen cookies

In addition to the contents of the jar, you will need to add the following ingredients:

½ cup butter, softened

1 egg

1 teaspoon vanilla extract

Dreamsicle Cookies

Preheat the oven to 375°F. In a large bowl, cream the butter, egg, and vanilla extract. Add the contents of the jar, and stir until well mixed. Drop the dough by heaping teaspoonfuls onto an ungreased baking sheet, spacing the cookies about 2 inches apart. Bake for 8 to 10 minutes or until light brown in color. Allow to cool for 5 minutes on the baking sheet. Then transfer to wire racks and cool completely. Serve immediately, or store in an airtight container for up to 2 weeks.

GINGERBREADCOOKIES

These mouth-watering cookies will fill your kitchen
with the tantalizing aroma of molasses and spice.

YIELD:
3 DOZEN COOKIES

JAR INGREDIENTS

3 ½ cups all-purpose
flour

I cup brown sugar

2 teaspoons ground
ginger

I teaspoon baking
powder

I teaspoon baking
soda

I teaspoon ground
cloves

I teaspoon ground
cinnamon

I teaspoon ground
allspice

ADDITIONAL
INGREDIENTS

¾ cup molasses

½ cup butter,
softened

I egg

1. Preheat the oven to 350°F.

2. Place all of the jar ingredients in a medium-sized bowl, and stir until well combined. Set aside.

3. Place the molasses, butter, and egg in a large bowl, and cream with an electric mixer set on low speed or with a fork.

4. Add the dry ingredients to the butter mixture, and blend with a mixer set on low speed or with a spoon until well combined.

5. Drop the dough by heaping teaspoonfuls onto an ungreased baking sheet, spacing the cookies about 2 inches apart to allow for spreading.

6. Bake for 10 to 12 minutes, or until light brown in color. Allow to cool for 5 minutes on the baking sheet. Then transfer to wire racks and cool completely.

7. Serve immediately, or store in an airtight container for up to 2 weeks.

CREATING THE JAR

2 cups all-purpose flour
1 teaspoon baking powder
1 teaspoon baking soda
1 cup brown sugar
2 teaspoons ground ginger
1 teaspoon ground cloves
1 teaspoon ground cinnamon
1 teaspoon ground allspice
1 ½ cups all-purpose flour

1. Wash and thoroughly dry a 1-quart wide-mouth canning jar.

2. Layer the ingredients in the jar as shown at left, pressing firmly with a flat-bottomed object, such as a tart tamper or the bottom of a narrow glass, after each addition. Make the layers as level as possible.

3. Secure the lid, and decorate as desired. (See page 22.) Attach the instructions for making the cookies found below.

Yield:
3 dozen cookies

In addition to the contents of the jar, you will need to add the following ingredients:

¾ cup molasses
½ cup butter, softened
1 egg

GINGERBREAD COOKIES

Preheat the oven to 350°F. In a large bowl, cream the molasses, butter, and egg. Add the contents of the jar, and stir until well mixed. Drop the dough by heaping teaspoonfuls onto an ungreased baking sheet, spacing the cookies about 2 inches apart. Bake for 10 to 12 minutes, or until light brown in color. Allow to cool for 5 minutes on the baking sheet. Then transfer to wire racks and cool completely. Serve immediately, or store in an airtight container for up to 2 weeks.

GORPCOOKIES
(Good Old Raisins and Peanuts)

JAR INGREDIENTS

1 ½ cups quick-cooking oatmeal

¾ cup all-purpose flour

½ cup brown sugar

¾ cup chopped unsalted peanuts

¾ cup dark raisins

¼ cup sugar

½ teaspoon baking soda

ADDITIONAL INGREDIENTS

⅔ cup butter, softened

1 egg

1 teaspoon vanilla extract

Instead of taking a snack mix to your next outing,
treat family and friends to these awesome cookies!

1. Preheat the oven to 350°F.

2. Place all of the jar ingredients in a medium-sized bowl, and stir until well combined. Set aside.

3. Place the butter, egg, and vanilla extract in a large bowl, and cream with an electric mixer set on low speed or with a fork.

4. Add the dry ingredients to the butter mixture, and blend with a mixer set on low speed or with a spoon until well combined.

5. Drop the dough by heaping teaspoonfuls onto an ungreased baking sheet, spacing the cookies about 2 inches apart to allow for spreading.

6. Bake for 8 to 10 minutes, or until light brown in color. Allow to cool for 5 minutes on the baking sheet. Then transfer to wire racks and cool completely.

7. Serve immediately, or store in an airtight container for up to 2 weeks.

CREATING THE JAR

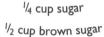

¼ cup sugar

½ cup brown sugar

¾ cup chopped unsalted peanuts

¾ cup dark raisins

1½ cups quick-cooking oatmeal

½ teaspoon baking soda

¾ cup all-purpose flour

1. Wash and thoroughly dry a 1-quart wide-mouth canning jar.

2. Layer the ingredients in the jar as shown at left, pressing firmly with a flat-bottomed object, such as a tart tamper or the bottom of a narrow glass, after each addition. Make the layers as level as possible.

3. Secure the lid, and decorate as desired. (See page 22.) Attach the instructions for making the cookies found below.

Yield:
3 dozen cookies

In addition to the contents of the jar, you will need to add the following ingredients:

⅔ cup butter, softened

1 egg

1 teaspoon vanilla extract

GORP COOKIES
(Good Old Raisins and Peanuts)

Preheat the oven to 350°F. In a large bowl, cream the butter, egg, and vanilla extract. Add the contents of the jar, and stir until well mixed. Drop the dough by heaping teaspoonfuls onto an ungreased baking sheet, spacing the cookies about 2 inches apart. Bake for 8 to 10 minutes or until light brown in color. Allow to cool for 5 minutes on the baking sheet. Then transfer to wire racks and cool completely. Serve immediately, or store in an airtight container for up to 2 weeks.

JELLYBEANGEMS

These little "gems" are a great way to use up
all those leftover Easter jelly beans!

YIELD:
3 DOZEN COOKIES

JAR INGREDIENTS

2 cups quick-cooking oatmeal

1 cup brown sugar

1 cup sugar

¾ cup jelly beans in assorted colors

1½ teaspoons baking soda

ADDITIONAL INGREDIENTS

½ cup creamy peanut butter

2 eggs

1. Preheat the oven to 350°F.

2. Place all of the jar ingredients in a medium-sized bowl, and stir until well combined. Set aside.

3. Place the peanut butter and eggs in a large bowl, and cream with an electric mixer set on low speed or with a fork.

4. Add the dry ingredients to the peanut butter mixture, and mix with a spoon until well combined.

5. Drop the dough by heaping teaspoonfuls onto an ungreased baking sheet, spacing the cookies about 2 inches apart to allow for spreading.

6. Bake for 10 to 12 minutes, or until light brown in color. Allow to cool for 5 minutes on the baking sheet. Then transfer to wire racks and cool completely.

7. Serve immediately, or store in an airtight container for up to 2 weeks.

CREATINGTHEJAR

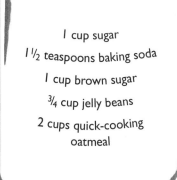

1 cup sugar
1½ teaspoons baking soda
1 cup brown sugar
¾ cup jelly beans
2 cups quick-cooking oatmeal

1. Wash and thoroughly dry a 1-quart wide-mouth canning jar.

2. Layer the ingredients in the jar as shown at left, pressing firmly with a flat-bottomed object, such as a tart tamper or the bottom of a narrow glass, after each addition. Make the layers as level as possible.

3. Secure the lid, and decorate as desired. (See page 22.) Attach the instructions for making the cookies found below.

Yield:
3 dozen cookies

In addition to the contents of the jar, you will need to add the following ingredients:

½ cup creamy peanut butter

2 eggs

JELLY BEAN GEMS

Preheat the oven to 350°F. In a large bowl, cream the peanut butter and eggs. Add the contents of the jar, and stir until well mixed. Drop the dough by heaping teaspoonfuls onto an ungreased baking sheet, spacing the cookies about 2 inches apart. Bake for 10 to 12 minutes or until light brown in color. Allow to cool for 5 minutes on the baking sheet. Then transfer to wire racks and cool completely. Serve immediately, or store in an airtight container for up to 2 weeks.

LEMONTHYMECOOKIES

If you don't grow lemon thyme in your own garden,
ask your favorite gardener to trade some for
a plate of these delicious cookies.

YIELD:
3 DOZEN COOKIES

JAR INGREDIENTS

2 ½ cups all-purpose
flour

1 ½ cups sugar

2 teaspoons cream
of tartar

½ teaspoon salt

**ADDITIONAL
INGREDIENTS**

1 cup butter, softened

2 eggs

½ cup chopped fresh
lemon thyme

1. Place all of the jar ingredients in a medium-sized bowl, and stir until well combined. Set aside.

2. Place the butter, eggs, and lemon thyme in a large bowl, and cream with an electric mixer set on low speed or with a fork.

3. Add the dry ingredients to the butter mixture, and blend with a mixer set on low speed or with a spoon until well combined. Cover the dough and chill it in the refrigerator for 2 hours.

4. Preheat the oven to 350°F.

5. Drop the dough by heaping teaspoonfuls onto an ungreased baking sheet, spacing the cookies about 2 inches apart to allow for spreading.

6. Bake for 9 to 11 minutes, or until light brown in color. Allow to cool for 5 minutes on the baking sheet. Then transfer to wire racks and cool completely.

7. Serve immediately, or store in an airtight container for up to 2 weeks.

CREATING THE JAR

1 1/2 cups sugar

2 1/2 cups all-purpose flour

1/2 teaspoon salt

2 teaspoons cream of tartar

1. Wash and thoroughly dry a 1-quart wide-mouth canning jar.

2. Layer the ingredients in the jar as shown at left, pressing firmly with a flat-bottomed object, such as a tart tamper or the bottom of a narrow glass, after each addition. Make the layers as level as possible.

3. Secure the lid, and decorate as desired. (See page 22.) Attach the instructions for making the cookies found below.

Yield:
3 dozen cookies

In addition to the contents of the jar, you will need to add the following ingredients:

1 cup butter, softened

2 eggs

1/2 cup chopped fresh lemon thyme

LEMON THYME COOKIES

In a large bowl, cream the butter, eggs, and lemon thyme. Add the contents of the jar, and stir until well mixed. Chill the dough for 2 hours. Preheat the oven to 350°F. Then drop the dough by heaping teaspoonfuls onto an ungreased baking sheet, spacing the cookies about 2 inches apart. Bake for 9 to 11 minutes or until light brown in color. Allow to cool for 5 minutes on the baking sheet. Then transfer to wire racks and cool completely. Serve immediately, or store in an airtight container for up to 2 weeks.

MILLIONBUCKSCOOKIES

Packed with walnuts and bits of luscious chocolate,
these cookies look and taste like a million bucks!

YIELD:
3 DOZEN COOKIES

JAR INGREDIENTS

1 1/4 cups quick-cooking oatmeal, blended fine in a blender

1 cup all-purpose flour

1/2 cup sugar

1/2 cup brown sugar

1/2 cup chopped walnuts

1/2 cup milk chocolate chips

1 bar (1.55 ounces) milk chocolate, chopped (about 1/2 cup)

1/2 teaspoon baking powder

1/2 teaspoon baking soda

ADDITIONAL INGREDIENTS

1/2 cup butter, softened

1 egg

1 teaspoon vanilla extract

1. Preheat the oven to 375°F.

2. Place all of the jar ingredients in a medium-sized bowl, and stir until well combined. Set aside.

3. Place the butter, egg, and vanilla extract in a large bowl, and cream with an electric mixer set on low speed or with a fork.

4. Add the dry ingredients to the butter mixture, and mix with a spoon until well combined.

5. Drop the dough by heaping teaspoonfuls onto an ungreased baking sheet, spacing the cookies about 2 inches apart to allow for spreading.

6. Bake for 8 to 10 minutes, or until light brown in color. Allow to cool for 5 minutes on the baking sheet. Then transfer to wire racks and cool completely.

7. Serve immediately, or store in an airtight container for up to 2 weeks.

CREATING THE JAR

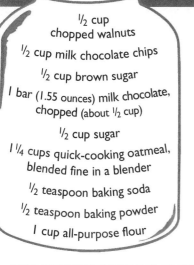

½ cup
chopped walnuts

½ cup milk chocolate chips

½ cup brown sugar

I bar (1.55 ounces) milk chocolate, chopped (about ½ cup)

½ cup sugar

1 ¼ cups quick-cooking oatmeal, blended fine in a blender

½ teaspoon baking soda

½ teaspoon baking powder

I cup all-purpose flour

1. Wash and thoroughly dry a 1-quart wide-mouth canning jar.

2. Layer the ingredients in the jar as shown at left, pressing firmly with a flat-bottomed object, such as a tart tamper or the bottom of a narrow glass, after each addition. Make the layers as level as possible.

3. Secure the lid, and decorate as desired. (See page 22.) Attach the instructions for making the cookies found below.

Yield:
3 dozen cookies

In addition to the contents of the jar, you will need to add the following ingredients:

½ cup butter, softened

I egg

I teaspoon vanilla extract

MILLION BUCKS COOKIES

Preheat the oven to 375°. In a large bowl, cream the butter, egg, and vanilla extract. Add the contents of the jar, and stir until well mixed. Drop the dough by heaping teaspoonfuls onto an ungreased baking sheet, spacing the cookies about 2 inches apart. Bake for 8 to 10 minutes, or until light brown in color. Allow to cool for 5 minutes on the baking sheet. Then transfer to wire racks and cool completely. Serve immediately, or store in an airtight container for up to 2 weeks.

MOCHA RUM BALLS

These easy no-bakes are a special treat during the holidays.

YIELD:
3 DOZEN COOKIES

JAR INGREDIENTS

2 cups crushed vanilla
wafers

1 1/4 cups powdered
sugar

1 cup finely chopped
almonds

2 tablespoons
unsweetened cocoa
powder

1 1/2 teaspoons instant
coffee granules

1/2 teaspoon ground
cinnamon

**ADDITIONAL
INGREDIENTS**

1/4 cup plus 1
tablespoon rum

3/4 cup powdered
sugar

1. Place all of the jar ingredients in a large bowl, and stir to mix. Add the rum to the dry ingredients, and stir until well combined.

2. Place the powdered sugar in a small bowl. Dust your hands with powdered sugar to prevent sticking, and form the dough into 2-inch balls. Roll each ball in the powdered sugar.

3. Arrange the balls in a single layer on a cookie sheet, and allow to air dry at room temperature for 6 hours.

4. Serve immediately, or store in an airtight container for up to 2 weeks.

CREATING THE JAR

1 cup finely
chopped almonds

2 cups crushed
vanilla wafers

1 1/4 cups powdered sugar

2 tablespoons
unsweetened cocoa powder

1 1/2 teaspoons
instant coffee granules

1/2 teaspoon
ground cinnamon

1. Wash and thoroughly dry a 1-quart wide-mouth canning jar.

2. Layer the ingredients in the jar as shown at left, pressing firmly with a flat-bottomed object, such as a tart tamper or the bottom of a narrow glass, after each addition. Make the layers as level as possible.

3. Secure the lid, and decorate as desired. (See page 22.) Attach the instructions for making the cookies found below.

Yield:
3 dozen cookies

In addition to the contents of the jar, you will need to add the following ingredients:

1/4 cup plus 1 tablespoon rum

3/4 cup powdered sugar

MOCHA RUM BALLS

In a large bowl, combine all of the jar ingredients. Add the rum and stir well to combine. Form the mixture into 2-inch balls. Place the powdered sugar in a bowl, and roll each ball in the sugar. Arrange the balls on a cookie sheet, and air dry at room temperature for 6 hours. Serve immediately, or store in an airtight container for up to 2 weeks.

MONSTERCOOKIES

Loaded with delicious ingredients—and colorful, too—
these cookies will be sure-fire winners
with all the cookie monsters in your home.

YIELD:
3¹/₂ DOZEN COOKIES

JAR INGREDIENTS

1¹/₄ cups quick-
cooking oatmeal

1 cup miniature candy-
coated chocolate
pieces, such as
M&M's Baking Bits

³/₄ cup all-purpose
flour

³/₄ cup brown sugar

¹/₂ cup chopped
walnuts

¹/₂ cup dark raisins

¹/₂ teaspoon salt

¹/₂ teaspoon ground
cinnamon

¹/₂ teaspoon baking
soda

**ADDITIONAL
INGREDIENTS**

³/₄ cup butter, softened

1 egg

1 teaspoon vanilla
extract

1. Preheat the oven to 350°F.

2. Place all of the jar ingredients in a medium-sized bowl, and stir until well combined. Set aside.

3. Place the butter, egg, and vanilla extract in a large bowl, and cream with an electric mixer set on low speed or with a fork.

4. Add the dry ingredients to the butter mixture, and mix with a spoon until well combined.

5. Drop the dough by heaping teaspoonfuls onto an ungreased baking sheet, spacing the cookies about 2 inches apart to allow for spreading.

6. Bake for 8 to 10 minutes, or until light brown in color. Allow to cool for 5 minutes on the baking sheet. Then transfer to wire racks and cool completely.

7. Serve immediately, or store in an airtight container for up to 2 weeks.

CREATINGTHEJAR

In the jar:

1¼ cups quick-cooking oatmeal

¾ cup brown sugar

½ cup dark raisins

1 cup miniature candy-coated chocolate pieces, such as M&M's Baking Bits

½ cup chopped walnuts

½ teaspoon ground cinnamon

½ teaspoon salt

½ teaspoon baking soda

¾ cup all-purpose flour

1. Wash and thoroughly dry a 1-quart wide-mouth canning jar.

2. Layer the ingredients in the jar as shown at left, pressing firmly with a flat-bottomed object, such as a tart tamper or the bottom of a narrow glass, after each addition. Make the layers as level as possible.

3. Secure the lid, and decorate as desired. (See page 22.) Attach the instructions for making the cookies found below.

Yield:
3½ dozen cookies

In addition to the contents of the jar, you will need to add the following ingredients:

¾ cup butter, softened

1 egg

1 teaspoon vanilla extract

MONSTER COOKIES

Preheat the oven to 350°F. In a large bowl, cream the butter, egg, and vanilla extract. Add the contents of the jar, and stir until well mixed. Drop the dough by heaping teaspoonfuls onto an ungreased baking sheet, spacing the cookies about 2 inches apart. Bake for 8 to 10 minutes or until light brown in color. Allow to cool for 5 minutes on the baking sheet. Then transfer to wire racks and cool completely. Serve immediately, or store in an airtight container for up to 2 weeks.

OATMEAL FRUIT COOKIES

Created for the health-conscious cookie lover, these treats are delicious enough to win raves from everyone—even kids.

YIELD:
2 DOZEN COOKIES

JAR INGREDIENTS

I cup all-purpose flour

I cup quick-cooking oatmeal

³/₄ cup wheat germ

²/₃ cup sweetened flaked coconut

¹/₂ cup golden raisins

¹/₂ cup dried cherries

¹/₂ cup brown sugar

¹/₄ cup sugar

¹/₂ teaspoon salt

¹/₂ teaspoon baking soda

ADDITIONAL INGREDIENTS

¹/₂ cup butter, softened

¹/₄ cup milk

I egg

I teaspoon vanilla extract

1. Preheat the oven to 350°F.

2. Place all of the jar ingredients in a medium-sized bowl, and stir until well combined. Set aside.

3. Place the butter, milk, egg, and vanilla extract in a large bowl, and cream with an electric mixer set on low speed or with a fork.

4. Add the dry ingredients to the butter mixture, and blend with a mixer set on low speed or with a spoon until well combined.

5. Drop the dough by heaping teaspoonfuls onto an ungreased baking sheet, spacing the cookies about 2 inches apart to allow for spreading.

6. Bake for 10 to 12 minutes, or until light brown in color. Allow to cool for 5 minutes on the baking sheet. Then transfer to wire racks and cool completely.

7. Serve immediately, or store in an airtight container for up to 2 weeks.

CREATINGTHEJAR

⅔ cup sweetened
flaked coconut

½ cup golden raisins

½ cup dried cherries

I cup quick-cooking oatmeal

¾ cup wheat germ

½ cup brown sugar

¼ cup sugar

½ teaspoon baking soda

½ teaspoon salt

I cup all-purpose flour

1. Wash and thoroughly dry a 1-quart wide-mouth canning jar.

2. Layer the ingredients in the jar as shown at left, pressing firmly with a flat-bottomed object, such as a tart tamper or the bottom of a narrow glass, after each addition. Make the layers as level as possible.

3. Secure the lid, and decorate as desired. (See page 22.) Attach the instructions for making the cookies found below.

Yield:
2 dozen cookies

In addition to the contents of the jar, you will need to add the following ingredients:

½ cup butter, softened

¼ cup milk

I egg

I teaspoon vanilla extract

OATMEAL FRUIT COOKIES

Preheat the oven to 350°F. In a large bowl, cream the butter, milk, egg, and vanilla extract. Add the contents of the jar, and stir until well mixed. Drop the dough by heaping teaspoonfuls onto an ungreased baking sheet, spacing the cookies about 2 inches apart. Bake for 10 to 12 minutes, or until light brown in color. Allow to cool for 5 minutes on the baking sheet. Then transfer to wire racks and cool completely. Serve immediately, or store in an airtight container for up to 2 weeks.

OLD-FASHIONED
SUGAR**COOKIES**

These cookies rate number-one with my kids. It's a tradition in our house to make these every Christmas. They usually don't last very long.

YIELD:
2 1/2 DOZEN COOKIES

JAR INGREDIENTS

3 cups all-purpose flour

1 1/2 cups sugar

1 teaspoon baking powder

1 teaspoon baking soda

1/8 teaspoon salt

ADDITIONAL INGREDIENTS

1 cup butter, softened

2 eggs

1 teaspoon vanilla extract

1/2 teaspoon lemon extract

1. Place all of the jar ingredients in a medium-sized bowl, and stir until well combined. Set aside.

2. Place the butter, eggs, and vanilla and lemon extracts in a large bowl, and cream with an electric mixer set on low speed or with a fork.

3. Add the dry ingredients to the butter mixture, and blend with a mixer set on low speed or with a spoon until well combined. Cover the dough and chill in the refrigerator for 2 hours.

4. Preheat the oven to 350°F.

5. On a lightly floured surface, roll the dough to 1/4-inch thickness. Cut into desired shapes with cookie cutters and arrange on an ungreased baking sheet, spacing the cookies about 2 inches apart to allow for spreading.

6. Bake for 10 to 12 minutes, or until the edges begin to brown. Allow to cool for 2 minutes on the baking sheet. Then transfer to wire racks and cool completely.

7. Serve immediately, or store in an airtight container for up to 2 weeks.

CREATING THE JAR

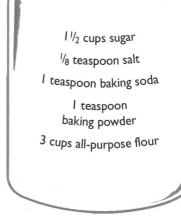

1 1/2 cups sugar

1/8 teaspoon salt

1 teaspoon baking soda

1 teaspoon baking powder

3 cups all-purpose flour

1. Wash and thoroughly dry a 1-quart wide-mouth canning jar.

2. Layer the ingredients in the jar as shown at left, pressing firmly with a flat-bottomed object, such as a tart tamper or the bottom of a narrow glass, after each addition. Make the layers as level as possible.

3. Secure the lid, and decorate as desired. (See page 22.) Attach the instructions for making the cookies found below.

Yield:
2 1/2 dozen cookies

In addition to the contents of the jar, you will need to add the following ingredients:

1 cup butter, softened

2 eggs

1 teaspoon vanilla extract

1/2 teaspoon lemon extract

OLD-FASHIONED SUGAR COOKIES

In a large bowl, cream the butter, eggs, and vanilla and lemon extracts. Add the contents of the jar, and stir until well mixed. Chill the dough for 2 hours. Preheat the oven to 350°F. On a lightly floured surface, roll the dough to 1/4-inch thickness. Cut into desired shapes with cookie cutters and place on an ungreased baking sheet, spacing the cookies about 2 inches apart. Bake for 10 to 12 minutes, or until the edges begin to brown. Allow to cool for 2 minutes on the baking sheet. Then transfer to wire racks and cool completely. Serve immediately, or store in an airtight container for up to 2 weeks.

ORANGEBURSTCOOKIES

To make orange rind slivers, peel off thin strips of the outer portion of an orange, avoiding the bitter white layer inside the rind. Cut the strips into thin slivers—and add a burst of fresh orange flavor to your cookies.

YIELD:
3 DOZEN COOKIES

JAR INGREDIENTS

3 ¼ cups all-purpose flour

1 ½ cups brown sugar

1 tablespoon freshly slivered orange rind

1 teaspoon baking powder

1 teaspoon baking soda

ADDITIONAL INGREDIENTS

½ cup butter, softened

¼ cup orange juice

2 eggs

1 teaspoon vanilla extract

1. Preheat the oven to 375°F.

2. Place all of the jar ingredients in a medium-sized bowl, and stir until well combined. Set aside.

3. Place the butter, orange juice, eggs, and vanilla extract in a large bowl, and cream with an electric mixer set on low speed or with a fork.

4. Add the dry ingredients to the butter mixture, and blend with a mixer set on low speed or with a spoon until well combined.

5. Drop the dough by heaping teaspoonfuls onto an ungreased baking sheet, spacing the cookies about 2 inches apart to allow for spreading.

6. Bake for 8 to 10 minutes, or until light brown in color. Allow to cool for 5 minutes on the baking sheet. Then transfer to wire racks and cool completely.

7. Serve immediately, or store in an airtight container for up to 2 weeks.

CREATING THE JAR

1½ cups brown sugar

1 tablespoon freshly slivered orange rind

1 teaspoon baking powder

1 teaspoon baking soda

3¼ cups all-purpose flour

1. Wash and thoroughly dry a 1-quart wide-mouth canning jar.

2. Layer the ingredients in the jar as shown at left, pressing firmly with a flat-bottomed object, such as a tart tamper or the bottom of a narrow glass, after each addition. Make the layers as level as possible.

3. Secure the lid, and decorate as desired. (See page 22.) Attach the instructions for making the cookies found below.

Yield: 3 dozen cookies

In addition to the contents of the jar, you will need to add the following ingredients:

½ cup butter, softened

¼ cup orange juice

2 eggs

1 teaspoon vanilla extract

ORANGE BURST COOKIES

Preheat the oven to 375°F. In a large bowl, cream the butter, orange juice, eggs, and vanilla extract. Add the contents of the jar, and stir until well mixed. Drop the dough by heaping teaspoonfuls onto an ungreased baking sheet, spacing the cookies about 2 inches apart. Bake for 8 to 10 minutes or until light brown in color. Allow to cool for 5 minutes on the baking sheet. Then transfer to wire racks and cool completely. Serve immediately, or store in an airtight container for up to 2 weeks.

ORANGESLICECOOKIES

*Orange slice candy adds both flavor and festive color
to these home-baked treats. To make the job of quartering
the candy easier, clean the knife between cuts by dipping
it in cold water and wiping it with a paper towel.*

YIELD:
2 1/2 DOZEN COOKIES

JAR INGREDIENTS

1 3/4 cups all-purpose
flour

3/4 cup sugar

1/2 cup brown sugar

20 pieces orange
slice candy, quartered
(1 1/2 cups, packed)

1 teaspoon baking
powder

1/2 teaspoon baking
soda

**ADDITIONAL
INGREDIENTS**

1/2 cup butter,
softened

2 eggs

1 teaspoon vanilla
extract

1. Preheat the oven to 375°F.

2. Place all of the jar ingredients in a medium-sized bowl, and stir until well combined. Set aside.

3. Place the butter, eggs, and vanilla extract in a large bowl, and cream with an electric mixer set on low speed or with a fork.

4. Add the dry ingredients to the butter mixture, and mix with a spoon until well combined.

5. Drop the dough by heaping teaspoonfuls onto an ungreased baking sheet, spacing the cookies about 2 inches apart to allow for spreading.

6. Bake for 9 to 12 minutes, or until light brown in color. Allow to cool for 5 minutes on the baking sheet. Then transfer to wire racks and cool completely.

7. Serve immediately, or store in an airtight container for up to 2 weeks.

CREATING THE JAR

20 pieces orange slice candy, quartered

½ cup brown sugar

¾ cup sugar

½ teaspoon baking soda

1 teaspoon baking powder

1¾ cups all-purpose flour

1. Wash and thoroughly dry a 1-quart wide-mouth canning jar.

2. Layer the ingredients in the jar as shown at left, pressing firmly with a flat-bottomed object, such as a tart tamper or the bottom of a narrow glass, after each addition. Make the layers as level as possible.

3. Secure the lid, and decorate as desired. (See page 22.) Attach the instructions for making the cookies found below.

Yield:
2½ dozen cookies

In addition to the contents of the jar, you will need to add the following ingredients:

½ cup butter, softened

2 eggs

1 teaspoon vanilla extract

ORANGE SLICE COOKIES

Preheat the oven to 375°F. In a large bowl, cream the butter, eggs, and vanilla extract. Add the contents of the jar, and stir until well mixed. Drop the dough by heaping teaspoonfuls onto an ungreased baking sheet, spacing the cookies about 2 inches apart. Bake for 9 to 12 minutes, or until light brown in color. Allow to cool for 5 minutes on the baking sheet. Then transfer to wire racks and cool completely. Serve immediately, or store in an airtight container for up to 2 weeks.

PARADISECOOKIES

YIELD:
2 1/2 DOZEN COOKIES

JAR INGREDIENTS

I cup all-purpose flour

I cup corn flakes

I cup quick-cooking oatmeal

3/4 cup brown sugar

3/4 cup semisweet chocolate chips

1/2 cup sugar

2 tablespoons sweetened flaked coconut

3/4 teaspoon baking soda

1/2 teaspoon baking powder

1/4 teaspoon salt

ADDITIONAL INGREDIENTS

1/2 cup butter, softened

I egg

I teaspoon vanilla extract

Get ready for a taste of paradise.
These cookies are loaded with incredible flavor.

1. Preheat the oven to 350°F.

2. Place all of the jar ingredients in a medium-sized bowl, and stir until well combined. Set aside.

3. Place the butter, egg, and vanilla extract in a large bowl, and cream with an electric mixer set on low speed or with a fork.

4. Add the dry ingredients to the butter mixture, and mix with a spoon until well combined.

5. Drop the dough by heaping teaspoonfuls onto an ungreased baking sheet, spacing the cookies about 2 inches apart to allow for spreading.

6. Bake for 10 to 12 minutes, or until light brown in color. Allow to cool for 5 minutes on the baking sheet. Then transfer to wire racks and cool completely.

7. Serve immediately, or store in an airtight container for up to 2 weeks.

CREATING THE JAR

¾ cup semisweet chocolate chips

I cup corn flakes

2 tablespoons sweetened flaked coconut

I cup quick-cooking oatmeal

¾ cup brown sugar

½ cup sugar

½ teaspoon baking powder

¾ teaspoon baking soda

¼ teaspoon salt

I cup all-purpose flour

1. Wash and thoroughly dry a 1-quart wide-mouth canning jar.

2. Layer the ingredients in the jar as shown at left, pressing firmly with a flat-bottomed object, such as a tart tamper or the bottom of a narrow glass, after each addition. Make the layers as level as possible.

3. Secure the lid, and decorate as desired. (See page 22.) Attach the instructions for making the cookies found below.

Yield:
2½ dozen cookies

In addition to the contents of the jar, you will need to add the following ingredients:

½ cup butter, softened

I egg

I teaspoon vanilla extract

PARADISE COOKIES

Preheat the oven to 350°F. In a large bowl, cream the butter, egg, and vanilla extract. Add the contents of the jar, and stir until well mixed. Drop the dough by heaping teaspoonfuls onto an ungreased baking sheet, spacing the cookies about 2 inches apart. Bake for 10 to 12 minutes, or until light brown in color. Allow to cool for 5 minutes on the baking sheet. Then transfer to wire racks and cool completely. Serve immediately, or store in an airtight container for up to 2 weeks.

PEANUTBUTTER**AND** CHOCOLATE**COOKIES**

*The combined flavors of peanut butter and chocolate chips
make these cookies similar to the popular candy cups.*

YIELD:
2 1/2 DOZEN COOKIES

JAR INGREDIENTS

1 3/4 cups all-purpose flour

3/4 cup sugar

1/2 cup brown sugar

1/2 cup peanut butter chips

1/2 cup semisweet chocolate chips

1 teaspoon baking powder

1/2 teaspoon baking soda

ADDITIONAL INGREDIENTS

1/2 cup butter, softened

1 egg

1 teaspoon vanilla extract

1. Preheat the oven to 375°F.

2. Place all of the jar ingredients in a medium-sized bowl, and stir until well combined. Set aside.

3. Place the butter, egg, and vanilla extract in a large bowl, and cream with an electric mixer set on low speed or with a fork.

4. Add the dry ingredients to the butter mixture, and mix with a spoon until well combined.

5. Drop the dough by heaping teaspoonfuls onto an ungreased baking sheet, spacing the cookies about 2 inches apart to allow for spreading.

6. Bake for 9 to 12 minutes, or until light brown in color. Allow to cool for 5 minutes on the baking sheet. Then transfer to wire racks and cool completely.

7. Serve immediately, or store in an airtight container for up to 2 weeks.

CREATING THE JAR

½ cup peanut butter
chips

½ cup semisweet
chocolate chips

½ teaspoon baking soda

I teaspoon baking powder

1¾ cups all-purpose flour

½ cup brown sugar

¾ cup sugar

1. Wash and thoroughly dry a 1-quart wide-mouth canning jar.

2. Layer the ingredients in the jar as shown at left, pressing firmly with a flat-bottomed object, such as a tart tamper or the bottom of a narrow glass, after each addition. Make the layers as level as possible.

3. Secure the lid, and decorate as desired. (See page 22.) Attach the instructions for making the cookies found below.

Yield:
2½ dozen cookies

In addition to the contents of the jar, you will need to add the following ingredients:

½ cup butter, softened

I egg

I teaspoon vanilla extract

PEANUT BUTTER AND CHOCOLATE COOKIES

Preheat the oven to 375°F. In a large bowl, cream the butter, egg, and vanilla extract. Add the contents of the jar, and stir until well mixed. Drop the dough by heaping teaspoonfuls onto an ungreased baking sheet, spacing the cookies about 2 inches apart. Bake for 9 to 12 minutes, or until light brown in color. Allow to cool for 5 minutes on the baking sheet. Then transfer to wire racks and cool completely. Serve immediately, or store in an airtight container for up to 2 weeks.

PEANUTBUTTER**COOKIES**

Next to Best Ever Chocolate Chip Cookies,
this classic is my favorite!

YIELD:
3 ¹/₂ DOZEN COOKIES

JAR INGREDIENTS

1 ³/₄ cups all-purpose flour

1 ¹/₄ cups brown sugar

1 cup chopped unsalted peanuts

³/₄ teaspoon baking soda

³/₄ teaspoon salt

ADDITIONAL INGREDIENTS

¹/₂ cup butter, softened

³/₄ cup smooth peanut butter

1 egg

3 tablespoons milk

1 tablespoon vanilla extract

¹/₄ cup sugar

1. Preheat the oven to 375°F.

2. Place all of the jar ingredients in a medium-sized bowl, and stir until well combined. Set aside.

3. Place the butter, peanut butter, egg, milk, and vanilla extract in a large bowl, and cream with an electric mixer set on low speed or with a fork.

4. Add the dry ingredients to the butter mixture, and blend with a mixer set on low speed or with a spoon until well combined.

5. Using your hands, form the dough into 2-inch balls. Place the ¹/₄ cup of sugar in a bowl, and roll the balls in the sugar to coat. Arrange the balls 2 inches apart on an ungreased baking sheet, and flatten each one with fork tines in a crisscross pattern, dipping the fork in sugar as necessary to prevent sticking.

6. Bake for 9 to 11 minutes, or until the edges are light brown in color. Allow to cool for 5 minutes on the baking sheet. Then transfer to wire racks and cool completely.

7. Serve immediately, or store in an airtight container for up to 2 weeks.

CREATING THE JAR

1 cup chopped
unsalted peanuts

¾ teaspoon salt

¾ teaspoon baking soda

1¼ cups brown sugar

1¾ cups all-purpose flour

1. Wash and thoroughly dry a 1-quart wide-mouth canning jar.

2. Layer the ingredients in the jar as shown at left, pressing firmly with a flat-bottomed object, such as a tart tamper or the bottom of a narrow glass, after each addition. Make the layers as level as possible.

3. Secure the lid, and decorate as desired. (See page 22.) Attach the instructions for making the cookies found below.

Yield:
3½ dozen cookies

In addition to the contents of the jar, you will need to add the following ingredients:

½ cup butter, softened

¾ cup smooth peanut butter

1 egg

3 tablespoons milk

1 tablespoon vanilla extract

¼ cup sugar

Peanut Butter Cookies
Preheat the oven to 375°F. In a large bowl, cream the butter, peanut butter, egg, milk, and vanilla extract. Add the contents of the jar, and stir until well mixed. Using your hands, form the dough into 2-inch balls. Roll the balls in the ¼ cup of sugar, and arrange them 2 inches apart on an ungreased baking sheet. Flatten each ball with fork tines in a crisscross pattern, and bake for 9 to 11 minutes, or until the edges are light brown in color. Allow to cool for 5 minutes on the baking sheet. Then transfer to wire racks and cool completely. Serve immediately, or store in an airtight container for up to 2 weeks.

PEANUTBUTTER**CUP** **COOKIES**

I had to put my favorite candy bar in a cookie. Enjoy!

YIELD:
3 DOZEN COOKIES

JAR INGREDIENTS

1¾ cups all-purpose flour

¾ cup sugar

½ cup brown sugar

1 teaspoon baking powder

½ teaspoon baking soda

8 peanut butter cups, coarsely chopped

ADDITIONAL INGREDIENTS

½ cup butter, softened

1 egg

1 teaspoon vanilla extract

1. Preheat the oven to 375°F.

2. Place all of the jar ingredients except for the peanut butter cups in a medium-sized bowl, and stir until well combined. Set aside.

3. Place the butter, egg, and vanilla extract in a large bowl, and cream with an electric mixer set on low speed or with a fork.

4. Add the dry ingredients to the butter mixture, and mix with a spoon until well combined. Stir in the peanut butter cups.

5. Drop the dough by heaping teaspoonfuls onto an ungreased baking sheet, spacing the cookies about 2 inches apart to allow for spreading.

6. Bake for 10 to 12 minutes, or until light brown in color. Allow to cool for 5 minutes on the baking sheet. Then transfer to wire racks and cool completely.

7. Serve immediately, or store in an airtight container for up to 2 weeks.

CREATING THE JAR

8 peanut butter cups, coarsely chopped

1/2 cup brown sugar

3/4 cup sugar

1/2 teaspoon baking soda

1 teaspoon baking powder

1 3/4 cups all-purpose flour

1. Wash and thoroughly dry a 1-quart wide-mouth canning jar.

2. Layer the ingredients in the jar as shown at left, pressing firmly with a flat-bottomed object, such as a tart tamper or the bottom of a narrow glass, after each addition. Make the layers as level as possible.

3. Secure the lid, and decorate as desired. (See page 22.) Attach the instructions for making the cookies found below.

Yield:
3 dozen cookies

In addition to the contents of the jar, you will need to add the following ingredients:

1/2 cup butter, softened

1 egg

1 teaspoon vanilla extract

PEANUT BUTTER CUP COOKIES
Preheat the oven to 375°F. In a large bowl, cream the butter, egg, and vanilla extract. Remove the peanut butter cups from the jar and set aside. Add the remaining contents of the jar to the butter mixture, and stir until well mixed. Stir in the peanut butter cups. Drop the dough by heaping teaspoonfuls onto an ungreased baking sheet, spacing the cookies about 2 inches apart. Bake for 10 to 12 minutes, or until light brown in color. Allow to cool for 5 minutes on the baking sheet. Then transfer to wire racks and cool completely. Serve immediately, or store in an airtight container for up to 2 weeks.

PECANCHOCOLATE**COOKIES**

Rich, chewy chocolate treats bursting with pecans,
these cookies appeal to nut lovers and chocolate lovers alike.

YIELD:
3 DOZEN COOKIES

JAR INGREDIENTS

1¾ cups all-purpose flour

1 cup sugar

1 cup chopped pecans

½ cup unsweetened cocoa powder

⅓ cup brown sugar

1 teaspoon baking soda

ADDITIONAL INGREDIENTS

½ cup butter, softened

1 egg

1 teaspoon vanilla extract

1. Preheat the oven to 375°F.

2. Place all of the jar ingredients in a medium-sized bowl, and stir until well combined. Set aside.

3. Place the butter, egg, and vanilla extract in a large bowl, and cream with an electric mixer set on low speed or with a fork.

4. Add the dry ingredients to the butter mixture, and blend with a mixer set on low speed or with a spoon until well combined.

5. Drop the dough by heaping teaspoonfuls onto an ungreased baking sheet, spacing the cookies about 2 inches apart to allow for spreading.

6. Bake for 9 to 11 minutes, or until light brown in color. Allow to cool for 5 minutes on the baking sheet. Then transfer to wire racks and cool completely.

7. Serve immediately, or store in an airtight container for up to 2 weeks.

CREATING THE JAR

I cup sugar

½ cup unsweetened cocoa powder

⅓ cup brown sugar

I cup chopped pecans

I teaspoon baking soda

1¾ cups all-purpose flour

1. Wash and thoroughly dry a 1-quart wide-mouth canning jar.

2. Layer the ingredients in the jar as shown at left, pressing firmly with a flat-bottomed object, such as a tart tamper or the bottom of a narrow glass, after each addition. Make the layers as level as possible.

3. Secure the lid, and decorate as desired. (See page 22.) Attach the instructions for making the cookies found below.

Yield:
3 dozen cookies

In addition to the contents of the jar, you will need to add the following ingredients:

½ cup butter, softened

I egg

I teaspoon vanilla extract

PECAN CHOCOLATE COOKIES

Preheat the oven to 375°F. In a large bowl, cream the butter, egg, and vanilla extract. Add the contents of the jar, and stir until well mixed. Drop the dough by heaping teaspoonfuls onto an ungreased baking sheet, spacing the cookies about 2 inches apart. Bake for 9 to 11 minutes, or until light brown in color. Allow to cool for 5 minutes on the baking sheet. Then transfer to wire racks and cool completely. Serve immediately, or store in an airtight container for up to 2 weeks.

PECANCOOKIES

To make a great gift for the nut lover in your life,
attach a nutcracker to the jarred mix of these delicious cookies.
Better yet, bake up a batch and prepare to bask in the compliments!

YIELD:
3 DOZEN COOKIES

JAR INGREDIENTS

1 1/4 cups quick-cooking oatmeal

1 cup crisped rice cereal

3/4 cup all-purpose flour

3/4 cup finely chopped pecans

1/2 cup sugar

1/2 cup brown sugar

1/2 teaspoon baking soda

1/2 teaspoon baking powder

ADDITIONAL INGREDIENTS

1/2 cup butter, softened

1 egg

1 teaspoon vanilla extract

1. Preheat the oven to 350°F.

2. Place all of the jar ingredients in a medium-sized bowl, and stir until well combined. Set aside.

3. Place the butter, egg, and vanilla extract in a large bowl, and cream with an electric mixer set on low speed or with a fork.

4. Add the dry ingredients to the butter mixture, and blend with a mixer set on low speed or with a spoon until well combined.

5. Drop the dough by heaping teaspoonfuls onto an ungreased baking sheet, spacing the cookies about 2 inches apart to allow for spreading.

6. Bake for 10 to 12 minutes, or until light brown in color. Allow to cool for 5 minutes on the baking sheet. Then transfer to wire racks and cool completely.

7. Serve immediately, or store in an airtight container for up to 2 weeks.

CREATING THE JAR

1 cup crisped rice cereal

¾ cup finely chopped pecans

1¼ cups quick-cooking oatmeal

½ cup brown sugar

½ cup sugar

½ teaspoon baking powder

½ teaspoon baking soda

¾ cup all-purpose flour

1. Wash and thoroughly dry a 1-quart wide-mouth canning jar.

2. Layer the ingredients in the jar as shown at left, pressing firmly with a flat-bottomed object, such as a tart tamper or the bottom of a narrow glass, after each addition. Make the layers as level as possible.

3. Secure the lid, and decorate as desired. (See page 22.) Attach the instructions for making the cookies found below.

Yield:
3 dozen cookies

In addition to the contents of the jar, you will need to add the following ingredients:

½ cup butter, softened

1 egg

1 teaspoon vanilla extract

PECAN COOKIES

Preheat the oven to 350°F. In a large bowl, cream the butter, egg, and vanilla extract. Add the contents of the jar, and stir until well mixed. Drop the dough by heaping teaspoonfuls onto an ungreased baking sheet, spacing the cookies about 2 inches apart. Bake for 10 to 12 minutes, or until light brown in color. Allow to cool for 5 minutes on the baking sheet. Then transfer to wire racks and cool completely. Serve immediately, or store in an airtight container for up to 2 weeks.

POTATOCHIPCOOKIES

*My Aunt Eleanor had a plate of these delicious cookies
on her kitchen table during my last visit.
When she told me they contained potato chips, I couldn't believe it!*

YIELD:
3 DOZEN COOKIES

JAR INGREDIENTS

2 1/2 cups all-purpose
flour

I cup crushed
potato chips

I cup sugar

2/3 cup chopped
pecans

I teaspoon baking
powder

**ADDITIONAL
INGREDIENTS**

1/2 cup butter,
softened

I egg

I teaspoon vanilla
extract

1. Preheat the oven to 350°F.

2. Place all of the jar ingredients in a medium-sized bowl, and stir until well combined. Set aside.

3. Place the butter, egg, and vanilla extract in a large bowl, and cream with an electric mixer set on low speed or with a fork.

4. Add the dry ingredients to the butter mixture, and blend with a mixer set on low speed or with a spoon until well combined.

5. Drop the dough by heaping teaspoonfuls onto an ungreased baking sheet, spacing the cookies about 2 inches apart to allow for spreading.

6. Bake for 12 to 14 minutes, or until light brown in color. Allow to cool for 5 minutes on the baking sheet. Then transfer to wire racks and cool completely.

7. Serve immediately, or store in an airtight container for up to 2 weeks.

CREATINGTHEJAR

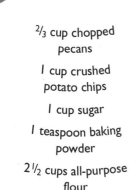

2/3 cup chopped
pecans

I cup crushed
potato chips

I cup sugar

I teaspoon baking
powder

2 1/2 cups all-purpose
flour

1. Wash and thoroughly dry a 1-quart wide-mouth canning jar.

2. Layer the ingredients in the jar as shown at left, pressing firmly with a flat-bottomed object, such as a tart tamper or the bottom of a narrow glass, after each addition. Make the layers as level as possible.

3. Secure the lid, and decorate as desired. (See page 22.) Attach the instructions for making the cookies found below.

Yield:
3 dozen cookies

In addition to the contents of the jar, you will need to add the following ingredients:

1/2 cup butter, softened

I egg

I teaspoon vanilla extract

POTATO CHIP COOKIES

Preheat the oven to 350°F. In a large bowl, cream the butter, egg, and vanilla extract. Add the contents of the jar, and stir until well mixed. Drop the dough by heaping teaspoonfuls onto an ungreased baking sheet, spacing the cookies about 2 inches apart. Bake for 12 to 14 minutes, or until light brown in color. Allow to cool for 5 minutes on the baking sheet. Then transfer to wire racks and cool completely. Serve immediately, or store in an airtight container for up to 2 weeks.

RAINBOWKIDSCOOKIES

*The colorful candies in the jarred mix create a rainbow
that any child would be delighted to receive.
And the finished cookies, rich with chocolate and brown sugar,
will be loved by children and adults alike.*

YIELD:
3 DOZEN COOKIES

JAR INGREDIENTS

1 cup quick-cooking oatmeal

1 cup all-purpose flour

1 cup brown sugar

3/4 cup miniature semisweet chocolate chips

1/2 cup miniature candy-coated chocolate pieces, such as M&M's Baking Bits

1/4 cup sugar

1 teaspoon baking soda

ADDITIONAL INGREDIENTS

1/2 cup butter, softened

1/2 cup smooth peanut butter

1 egg

1 teaspoon vanilla extract

1. Preheat the oven to 375°F.

2. Place all of the jar ingredients in a medium-sized bowl, and stir until well combined. Set aside.

3. Place the butter, peanut butter, egg, and vanilla extract in a large bowl, and cream with an electric mixer set on low speed or with a fork.

4. Add the dry ingredients to the butter mixture, and mix with a spoon until well combined.

5. Drop the dough by heaping teaspoonfuls onto an ungreased baking sheet, spacing the cookies about 2 inches apart to allow for spreading.

6. Bake for 11 to 13 minutes, or until light brown in color. Allow to cool for 5 minutes on the baking sheet. Then transfer to wire racks and cool completely.

7. Serve immediately, or store in an airtight container for up to 2 weeks.

CREATINGTHEJAR

³/₄ cup miniature semisweet chocolate chips

¹/₂ cup miniature candy-coated chocolate pieces, such as M&M's Baking Bits

1 teaspoon baking soda

¹/₂ cup quick-cooking oatmeal

¹/₂ cup brown sugar

¹/₂ cup quick-cooking oatmeal

¹/₄ cup sugar

¹/₂ cup brown sugar

1 cup all-purpose flour

1. Wash and thoroughly dry a 1-quart wide-mouth canning jar.

2. Layer the ingredients in the jar as shown at left, pressing firmly with a flat-bottomed object, such as a tart tamper or the bottom of a narrow glass, after each addition. Make the layers as level as possible.

3. Secure the lid, and decorate as desired. (See page 22.) Attach the instructions for making the cookies found below.

Yield: 3 dozen cookies

In addition to the contents of the jar, you will need to add the following ingredients:

¹/₂ cup butter, softened

¹/₂ cup smooth peanut butter

1 egg

1 teaspoon vanilla extract

RAINBOW KIDS COOKIES

Preheat the oven to 375°F. In a large bowl, cream the butter, peanut butter, egg, and vanilla extract. Add the contents of the jar, and stir until well mixed. Drop the dough by heaping teaspoonfuls onto an ungreased baking sheet, spacing the cookies about 2 inches apart. Bake for 11 to 13 minutes, or until light brown in color. Allow to cool for 5 minutes on the baking sheet. Then transfer to wire racks and cool completely. Serve immediately, or store in an airtight container for up to 2 weeks.

SNICKERDOODLES

Soft and cinnamony, these rich cookies are a universal favorite.

YIELD:
3 DOZEN COOKIES

JAR INGREDIENTS

2 3/4 cups all-purpose
flour

1 1/2 cups sugar

2 teaspoons cream of
tartar

1 teaspoon baking
soda

1/4 teaspoon salt

**ADDITIONAL
INGREDIENTS**

1 cup butter, softened

2 eggs

1/2 cup sugar

1 tablespoon ground
cinnamon

1. Preheat the oven to 350°F.

2. Place all of the jar ingredients in a medium-sized bowl, and stir until well combined. Set aside.

3. Place the butter and eggs in a large bowl, and cream with an electric mixer set on low speed or with a fork.

4. Add the dry ingredients to the butter mixture, and blend with a mixer set on low speed or with a spoon until well combined.

5. Form the dough into 1-inch balls. Combine the remaining sugar and the cinnamon in a small bowl, and roll each of the balls in the sugar mixture.

6. Arrange the balls on an ungreased baking sheet, spacing them about 2 inches apart to allow for spreading.

7. Bake for 12 to 15 minutes, or until the edges are light brown in color. Allow to cool for 5 minutes on the baking sheet. Then transfer to wire racks and cool completely.

8. Serve immediately, or store in an airtight container for up to 2 weeks.

CREATINGTHEJAR

1 1/2 cups sugar

2 teaspoons cream of tartar

1 teaspoon baking soda

1/4 teaspoon salt

2 3/4 cups all-purpose flour

1. Wash and thoroughly dry a 1-quart wide-mouth canning jar.

2. Layer the ingredients in the jar as shown at left, pressing firmly with a flat-bottomed object, such as a tart tamper or the bottom of a narrow glass, after each addition. Make the layers as level as possible.

3. Secure the lid, and decorate as desired. (See page 22.) Attach the instructions for making the cookies found below.

Yield:
3 dozen cookies

In addition to the contents of the jar, you will need to add the following ingredients:

1 cup butter, softened

2 eggs

1/2 cup sugar

1 tablespoon ground cinnamon

SNICKERDOODLES   Preheat the oven to 350°F. In a large bowl, cream the butter and eggs. Add the contents of the jar, and stir until well mixed. Form the dough into 1-inch balls. Combine the remaining sugar and the cinnamon in a small bowl, and roll each ball in the mixture. Arrange the balls on an ungreased baking sheet, spacing them about 2 inches apart. Bake for 12 to 15 minutes, or until the edges are light brown in color. Allow to cool for 5 minutes on the baking sheet. Then transfer to wire racks and cool completely. Serve immediately, or store in an airtight container for up to 2 weeks.

SNOWBALLS

In my house, Christmas wouldn't be the same without
these delicate little cookies. Simply roll the warm cookie balls
in powdered sugar to give this classic a snowball effect.

YIELD:
3 DOZEN COOKIES

JAR INGREDIENTS

2 cups all-purpose
flour

1 cup chopped
pecans

1/3 cup powdered
sugar

**ADDITIONAL
INGREDIENTS**

1 cup butter, softened

2 teaspoons water

2 teaspoons vanilla
extract

1/2 cup powdered
sugar

1. Preheat the oven to 325°F.

2. Place all of the jar ingredients in a medium-sized bowl, and stir until well combined. Set aside.

3. Place the butter, water, and vanilla extract in a large bowl, and cream with an electric mixer set on low speed or with a fork.

4. Add the dry ingredients to the butter mixture, and blend with a mixer set on low speed or with a spoon until well combined. Cover the dough and chill for 4 hours.

5. Form the dough into 1-inch balls and arrange them on an ungreased baking sheet, spacing them about 2 inches apart to allow for spreading.

6. Bake for 20 to 25 minutes, or until slightly brown on the bottom. Remove the cookies from the baking sheet, and roll each ball in the remaining powdered sugar while still warm. Then transfer to wire racks and cool completely.

7. Serve immediately, or store in an airtight container for up to 2 weeks.

CREATING THE JAR

1 cup chopped pecans

1/3 cup powdered sugar

2 cups all-purpose flour

1. Wash and thoroughly dry a 1-quart wide-mouth canning jar.

2. Layer the ingredients in the jar as shown at left, pressing firmly with a flat-bottomed object, such as a tart tamper or the bottom of a narrow glass, after each addition. Make the layers as level as possible.

3. Secure the lid, and decorate as desired. (See page 22.) Attach the instructions for making the cookies found below.

Yield: 3 dozen cookies

In addition to the contents of the jar, you will need to add the following ingredients:

1 cup butter, softened

2 teaspoons water

2 teaspoons vanilla extract

1/2 cup powdered sugar

SNOWBALLS Preheat the oven to 325°F. In a large bowl, cream the butter, water, and vanilla extract. Add the contents of the jar, and stir until well mixed. Chill the dough for 4 hours. Then form into 1-inch balls, and arrange the balls on an ungreased baking sheet, spacing them about 2 inches apart. Bake for 20 to 25 minutes, or until slightly brown on the bottom. Remove the cookies from the baking sheet, and roll in the remaining powdered sugar while still warm. Then transfer to wire racks and cool completely. Serve immediately, or store in an airtight container for up to 2 weeks.

TRAIL MIX COOKIES

This recipe combines nutritious ingredients to make a treat
that is both healthy and delicious.

YIELD:
2 1/2 DOZEN COOKIES

JAR INGREDIENTS

3/4 cup all-purpose
flour

3/4 cup wheat germ

1/2 cup sugar

1/2 cup brown sugar

1/2 cup dried
cranberries

1/2 cup dark raisins

1/2 cup chopped
pecans

1/3 cup quick-cooking
oatmeal

1/3 cup sweetened
flaked coconut

I teaspoon baking
powder

ADDITIONAL
INGREDIENTS

1/2 cup butter,
softened

I egg

I teaspoon vanilla
extract

1. Preheat the oven to 350°.

2. Place all of the jar ingredients in a medium-sized bowl, and stir until well combined. Set aside.

3. Place the butter, egg, and vanilla extract in a large bowl, and cream with an electric mixer set on low speed or with a fork.

4. Add the dry ingredients to the butter mixture, and mix with a spoon until well combined.

5. Drop the dough by heaping teaspoonfuls onto an ungreased baking sheet, spacing the cookies about 2 inches apart to allow for spreading.

6. Bake for 12 to 14 minutes, or until light brown in color. Allow to cool for 5 minutes on the baking sheet. Then transfer to wire racks and cool completely.

7. Serve immediately, or store in an airtight container for up to 2 weeks.

CREATINGTHEJAR

½ cup chopped pecans

½ cup dark raisins

½ cup dried cranberries

⅓ cup sweetened flaked coconut

⅓ cup quick-cooking oatmeal

¾ cup wheat germ

½ cup brown sugar

½ cup sugar

1 teaspoon baking powder

¾ cup all-purpose flour

1. Wash and thoroughly dry a 1-quart wide-mouth canning jar.

2. Layer the ingredients in the jar as shown at left, pressing firmly with a flat-bottomed object, such as a tart tamper or the bottom of a narrow glass, after each addition. Make the layers as level as possible.

3. Secure the lid, and decorate as desired. (See page 22.) Attach the instructions for making the cookies found below.

Yield:
2½ dozen cookies

In addition to the contents of the jar, you will need to add the following ingredients:

½ cup butter, softened

1 egg

1 teaspoon vanilla extract

TRAIL MIX COOKIES

Preheat the oven to 350°F. In a large bowl, cream the butter, egg, and vanilla extract. Add the contents of the jar, and stir until well mixed. Drop the dough by heaping teaspoonfuls onto an ungreased baking sheet, spacing the cookies about 2 inches apart. Bake for 12 to 14 minutes, or until light brown in color. Allow to cool for 5 minutes on the baking sheet. Then transfer to wire racks and cool completely. Serve immediately, or store in an airtight container for up to 2 weeks.

ULTIMATECHOCOLATE OATMEALCOOKIES

These cookies are rich, chewy,
and bursting with nuts and chocolate.

1. Preheat the oven to 375°F.

2. Place all of the jar ingredients in a medium-sized bowl, and stir until well combined. Set aside.

3. Place the butter, egg, and vanilla extract in a large bowl, and cream with an electric mixer set on low speed or with a fork.

4. Add the dry ingredients to the butter mixture, and mix with a spoon until well combined.

5. Drop the dough by heaping teaspoonfuls onto an ungreased baking sheet, spacing the cookies about 2 inches apart to allow for spreading.

6. Bake for 8 to 10 minutes, or until light brown in color. Allow to cool for 5 minutes on the baking sheet. Then transfer to wire racks and cool completely.

7. Serve immediately, or store in an airtight container for up to 2 weeks.

CREATING THE JAR

½ cup semisweet chocolate chips

½ cup chopped pecans

½ cup brown sugar

I bar (1.55 ounces) milk chocolate, grated (about ½ cup)

½ cup sugar

1 ¼ cups quick-cooking oatmeal, blended fine in a blender

½ teaspoon baking soda

½ teaspoon baking powder

I cup all-purpose flour

1. Wash and thoroughly dry a 1-quart wide-mouth canning jar.

2. Layer the ingredients in the jar as shown at left, pressing firmly with a flat-bottomed object, such as a tart tamper or the bottom of a narrow glass, after each addition. Make the layers as level as possible.

3. Secure the lid, and decorate as desired. (See page 22.) Attach the instructions for making the cookies found below.

Yield:
3 dozen cookies

In addition to the contents of the jar, you will need to add the following ingredients:

½ cup butter, softened

I egg

I teaspoon vanilla extract

ULTIMATE CHOCOLATE OATMEAL COOKIES

Preheat the oven to 375°F. In a large bowl, cream the butter, egg, and vanilla extract. Add the contents of the jar, and stir until well mixed. Drop the dough by heaping teaspoonfuls onto an ungreased baking sheet, spacing the cookies about 2 inches apart. Bake for 8 to 10 minutes or until light brown in color. Allow to cool for 5 minutes on the baking sheet. Then transfer to wire racks and cool completely. Serve immediately, or store in an airtight container for up to 2 weeks.

WHITECHOCOLATE
MACADAMIANUTCOOKIES

YIELD:
2 1/2 DOZEN COOKIES

Bake up a batch of these cookies,
and sink your teeth into a rich, buttery piece of heaven!

JAR INGREDIENTS

2 cups all-purpose flour

1 1/4 cups sugar

1/2 cup chopped macadamia nuts

1 bar (1.55 ounces) white chocolate, chopped (about 1/2 cup)

1/2 teaspoon baking soda

1/2 teaspoon baking powder

ADDITIONAL INGREDIENTS

1/2 cup butter, softened

1 egg

1 teaspoon vanilla extract

1. Preheat the oven to 375°F.

2. Place all of the jar ingredients in a medium-sized bowl, and stir until well combined. Set aside.

3. Place the butter, egg, and vanilla extract in a large bowl, and cream with an electric mixer set on low or with a fork.

4. Add the dry ingredients to the butter mixture, and mix with a spoon until well combined.

5. Drop the dough by heaping teaspoonfuls onto an ungreased baking sheet, spacing the cookies about 2 inches apart to allow for spreading.

6. Bake for 10 to 12 minutes, or until light brown in color. Allow to cool for 5 minutes on the baking sheet. Then transfer to wire racks and cool completely.

7. Serve immediately, or store in an airtight container for up to 2 weeks.

CREATING THE JAR

½ cup chopped
macadamia nuts

I bar (1.55 ounces)
white chocolate, chopped
(about ½ cup)

1¼ cups sugar

½ teaspoon baking powder

½ teaspoon baking soda

2 cups all-purpose flour

1. Wash and thoroughly dry a 1-quart wide-mouth canning jar.

2. Layer the ingredients in the jar as shown at left, pressing firmly with a flat-bottomed object, such as a tart tamper or the bottom of a narrow glass, after each addition. Make the layers as level as possible.

3. Secure the lid, and decorate as desired. (See page 22.) Attach the instructions for making the cookies found below.

Yield:
2½ dozen cookies

In addition to the contents of the jar, you will need to add the following ingredients:

½ cup butter, softened

I egg

I teaspoon vanilla extract

WHITE CHOCOLATE MACADAMIA NUT COOKIES

Preheat the oven to 375°F. In a large bowl, cream the butter, egg, and vanilla extract. Add the contents of the jar, and stir until well mixed. Drop the dough by heaping teaspoonfuls onto an ungreased baking sheet, spacing the cookies about 2 inches apart. Bake for 10 to 12 minutes, or until light brown in color. Allow to cool for 5 minutes on the baking sheet. Then transfer to wire racks and cool completely. Serve immediately, or store in an airtight container for up to 2 weeks.

Brownieand **Bar**Recipes

BLONDIES

Somewhere between a brownie and a chocolate chip cookie,
a blondie is a rich vanilla-flavored bar cookie
studded with chocolate bits and nuts. Luscious!

YIELD:
9 BARS

JAR INGREDIENTS

1 1/2 cups semisweet
chocolate chips

1 cup all-purpose
flour

1 cup brown sugar

1/2 cup coarsely
chopped walnuts

1/2 teaspoon salt

1/2 teaspoon baking
powder

1/8 teaspoon baking
soda

ADDITIONAL
INGREDIENTS

1/3 cup melted butter,
slightly cooled

1 egg

1 teaspoon vanilla
extract

1. Preheat the oven to 350°F. Grease a 9-x-9-inch baking pan, and set aside.

2. Place all of the jar ingredients in a medium-sized bowl, and stir until well combined. Set aside.

3. Place the butter, egg, and vanilla extract in a large bowl, and stir until well mixed.

4. Add the dry ingredients to the butter mixture, and mix with a spoon until well combined.

5. Spread the batter evenly in the prepared pan and bake for 18 to 20 minutes, or until golden brown in color.

6. Cool completely in the pan before cutting into bars. Serve immediately, or store in an airtight container for up to 2 weeks.

CREATINGTHEJAR

1½ cups semisweet chocolate chips

½ cup coarsely chopped walnuts

1 cup brown sugar

½ teaspoon salt

⅛ teaspoon baking soda

½ teaspoon baking powder

1 cup all-purpose flour

1. Wash and thoroughly dry a 1-quart wide-mouth canning jar.

2. Layer the ingredients in the jar as shown at left, pressing firmly with a flat-bottomed object, such as a tart tamper or the bottom of a narrow glass, after each addition. Make the layers as level as possible.

3. Secure the lid, and decorate as desired. (See page 22.) Attach the instructions for making the cookies found below.

Yield:
9 bars

In addition to the contents of the jar, you will need to add the following ingredients:

⅓ cup melted butter, slightly cooled

1 egg

1 teaspoon vanilla extract

BLONDIES

Preheat the oven to 350°F. Place the melted butter, egg, and vanilla extract in a large bowl, and stir to combine. Add the contents of the jar, and stir until well mixed. Spread the batter in a greased 9-x-9-inch baking pan and bake for 18 to 20 minutes, or until golden brown in color. Cool completely in the pan before cutting into bars. Serve immediately, or store in an airtight container for up to 2 weeks.

BUTTERNUTCHEWYBARS

*These buttery bars are special enough for company, but so easy to make
that you'll be able to whip up a batch any time.*

YIELD:
2 DOZEN BARS

JAR INGREDIENTS

2 cups brown sugar

1 ½ cups all-purpose
flour

1 cup chopped
pecans

2 teaspoons baking
powder

**ADDITIONAL
INGREDIENTS**

½ cup butter,
softened

2 eggs

1 teaspoon vanilla
extract

1. Preheat the oven to 350°F. Generously grease a 13-x-9-inch baking pan, and set aside.

2. Place all of the jar ingredients in a medium-sized bowl, and stir until well combined. Set aside.

3. Place the butter, eggs, and vanilla extract in a large bowl, and cream with an electric mixer set on low speed or with a fork.

4. Add the dry ingredients to the butter mixture, and mix with a spoon until well combined.

5. Spread the batter evenly in the prepared pan and bake for 25 to 30 minutes, or until the edges are light brown in color.

6. Cool completely in the pan before cutting into bars. Serve immediately, or store in an airtight container for up to 1 week.

CREATING THE JAR

1 cup chopped pecans

1 cup brown sugar

2 teaspoons baking powder

1 1/2 cups all-purpose flour

1 cup brown sugar

1. Wash and thoroughly dry a 1-quart wide-mouth canning jar.

2. Layer the ingredients in the jar as shown at left, pressing firmly with a flat-bottomed object, such as a tart tamper or the bottom of a narrow glass, after each addition. Make the layers as level as possible.

3. Secure the lid, and decorate as desired. (See page 22.) Attach the instructions for making the cookies found below.

Yield:
2 dozen bars

In addition to the contents of the jar, you will need to add the following ingredients:

1/2 cup butter, softened

2 eggs

1 teaspoon vanilla extract

BUTTER NUT CHEWY BARS

Preheat the oven to 350°F. In a large bowl, cream the butter, eggs, and vanilla extract. Add the contents of the jar, and stir until well mixed. Spread the batter evenly in a generously greased 13-x-9-inch baking pan and bake for 25 to 30 minutes, or until the edges are light brown in color. Cool completely in the pan before cutting into bars. Serve immediately, or store in an airtight container for up to 1 week.

CHOCOLATEORANGE OATFINGERBARS

YIELD:
9 BARS

These easy-to-prepare bars make a delicious snack. Just be sure to cool them completely before cutting and serving.

JAR INGREDIENTS

2 cups quick-cooking oatmeal

I cup miniature semisweet chocolate chips

$^2/_3$ cup brown sugar

2 tablespoons all-purpose flour

2 tablespoons grated orange peel

ADDITIONAL INGREDIENTS

$^1/_2$ cup melted butter, slightly cooled

3 tablespoons corn syrup

2 tablespoons honey

2 tablespoons orange juice

1. Preheat the oven to 350°F. Grease a 9-x-9-inch baking pan, and set aside.

2. Place all of the jar ingredients in a medium-sized bowl, and stir until well combined. Set aside.

3. Place the melted butter, corn syrup, honey, and orange juice in a large bowl, and stir to mix.

4. Add the dry ingredients to the butter mixture, and mix with a spoon until well combined.

5. Spread the batter evenly in the prepared pan and bake for 20 to 25 minutes, or until the edges of the bars are light brown in color.

6. Cool completely in the pan before cutting into bars. Serve immediately, or store in an airtight container for up to 1 week.

CREATINGTHEJAR

I cup miniature semisweet chocolate chips

²⁄₃ cup brown sugar

2 tablespoons all-purpose flour

2 tablespoons grated orange peel

2 cups quick-cooking oatmeal

1. Wash and thoroughly dry a 1-quart wide-mouth canning jar.

2. Layer the ingredients in the jar as shown at left, pressing firmly with a flat-bottomed object, such as a tart tamper or the bottom of a narrow glass, after each addition. Make the layers as level as possible.

3. Secure the lid, and decorate as desired. (See page 22.) Attach the instructions for making the cookies found below.

Yield: 9 bars

In addition to the contents of the jar, you will need to add the following ingredients:

½ cup melted butter, slightly cooled

3 tablespoons corn syrup

2 tablespoons honey

2 tablespoons orange juice

Chocolate Orange Oat Finger Bars

Preheat the oven to 350°F. Place the butter, corn syrup, honey, and orange juice in a large bowl, and stir to combine. Add the contents of the jar, and stir until well mixed. Spread the batter in a greased 9-x-9-inch baking pan and bake for 20 to 25 minutes, or until the edges of the bars are light brown in color. Cool completely in the pan before cutting into bars. Serve immediately, or store in an airtight container for up to 1 week.

GOOEYTURTLEBARS

*These delicious chocolate and caramel bars are a snap to make—
and they're so good!*

YIELD:
9 BARS

JAR INGREDIENTS

1½ cups vanilla wafer
crumbs

2 cups semisweet
chocolate chips

1 cup coarsely
chopped pecans

**ADDITIONAL
INGREDIENTS**

½ cup melted butter,
slightly cooled

1 jar (11.75 ounces)
caramel topping

1. Preheat the oven to 350°F.

2. Place the vanilla wafer crumbs and melted butter in a medium-sized bowl, and mix well with a fork. Transfer the crumb mixture to an ungreased 9-x-9-inch baking pan and, using the back of a fork, press the mixture firmly over the bottom and sides of the pan. Sprinkle the chocolate chips and pecans evenly over the crumb mixture.

3. Place the caramel topping in a microwave-safe bowl, and microwave on high power for 1½ minutes, or until the topping has a thin consistency. Alternatively, place the topping in a small saucepan and cook over low heat, stirring constantly. Drizzle the topping over the chocolate chips and pecans.

4. Bake for 12 to 15 minutes, or until the edges are light brown in color. Cool at room temperature for 30 minutes. Then chill in the refrigerator for 30 minutes.

5. Cut into bars and serve immediately, or store in an airtight container in the refrigerator for up to 2 weeks.

CREATING THE JAR

2 cups semisweet chocolate chips

1 cup coarsely chopped pecans

1 1/2 cups vanilla wafer crumbs

1. Wash and thoroughly dry a 1-quart wide-mouth canning jar.

2. Layer the ingredients in the jar as shown at left, pressing firmly with a flat-bottomed object, such as a tart tamper or the bottom of a narrow glass, after each addition. Make the layers as level as possible.

3. Secure the lid, and decorate as desired. (See page 22.) Attach the instructions for making the cookies found below.

Yield:
9 bars

In addition to the contents of the jar, you will need to add the following ingredients:

1/2 cup melted butter, slightly cooled

1 jar (11.75 ounces) caramel topping

GOOEY TURTLE BARS

Preheat the oven to 350°F. Remove the chocolate chips and pecans from the jar, and set aside. In a medium-sized bowl, combine the vanilla wafer crumbs with the melted butter. Transfer the mixture to an ungreased 9-x-9-inch baking pan, and use the back of a fork to press firmly over the bottom and sides of the pan. Sprinkle the chocolate chips and pecans evenly over the crumb mixture. Cook the caramel topping in a microwave oven for 1 1/2 minutes on high power, or cook on a conventional stovetop over low heat until thin in consistency. Drizzle the topping over the chocolate chips and pecans and bake for 12 to 15 minutes, or until the edges are light brown. Cool at room temperature for 30 minutes; then refrigerate for 30 minutes. Cut into bars and serve immediately, or refrigerate in an airtight container for up to 2 weeks.

MAGICCOOKIEBARS

If you want to know what's magical about these bars,
mix up a batch and watch them disappear before your eyes.

YIELD:
2 DOZEN BARS

JAR INGREDIENTS

1 1/2 cups graham cracker crumbs

1 cup sweetened flaked coconut

3/4 cup semisweet chocolate chips

3/4 cup butterscotch chips

1/2 cup coarsely chopped walnuts

ADDITIONAL INGREDIENTS

1/2 cup melted butter, slightly cooled

1 can (14 ounces) sweetened condensed milk

1. Preheat the oven to 350°F.

2. Place the graham cracker crumbs and melted butter in a medium-sized bowl, and mix well with a fork. Transfer the mixture to an ungreased 13-x-9-inch baking pan and, using the back of the fork, press the mixture firmly over the bottom of the pan and slightly up the sides.

3. Place all of the remaining jar ingredients in a medium-sized bowl, and stir to combine well. Sprinkle the mixture evenly over the graham cracker mixture. Then pour the sweetened condensed milk evenly over all.

4. Bake for 25 to 30 minutes, or until the edges are light brown in color.

5. Cool completely in the pan before cutting into bars. Serve immediately, or store in an airtight container in the refrigerator for up to 1 week.

CREATINGTHEJAR

¾ cup semisweet
chocolate chips

¾ cup butterscotch chips

½ cup coarsely chopped
walnuts

I cup sweetened
flaked coconut

I ½ cups graham cracker
crumbs

1. Wash and thoroughly dry a 1-quart wide-mouth canning jar.

2. Layer the ingredients in the jar as shown at left, pressing firmly with a flat-bottomed object, such as a tart tamper or the bottom of a narrow glass, after each addition. Make the layers as level as possible.

3. Secure the lid, and decorate as desired. (See page 22.) Attach the instructions for making the cookies found below.

Yield:
2 dozen bars

In addition to the contents of the jar, you will need to add the following ingredients:

½ cup melted butter,
slightly cooled

I can (14 ounces) sweetened
condensed milk

MAGIC COOKIE BARS   Preheat the oven to 350°F.
Spoon out all of the ingredients except for the graham cracker crumbs. Place the crumbs in a medium-sized bowl, and combine with the melted butter, stirring with a fork. Transfer the mixture to an ungreased 13-x-9-inch baking pan, and use the back of a fork to press it firmly over the bottom of the pan and slightly up the sides. Stir the remaining jar ingredients to combine, and sprinkle evenly over the crumb mixture. Then pour the sweetened condensed milk evenly over all. Bake for 25 to 30 minutes, or until the edges are light brown in color. Cool completely in the pan before cutting into bars. Serve immediately, or refrigerate in an airtight container for up to 1 week.

MOM'S BREAKFAST BARS

No time to stop for breakfast? Keep some of these
easy no-bake bars on hand and you'll be able to take
breakfast with you to work, to school, or on errands.

YIELD:
9 BARS

JAR INGREDIENTS

2 cups crisped rice cereal

1 cup semisweet chocolate chips

1 cup corn flakes

ADDITIONAL INGREDIENTS

½ cup light corn syrup

¼ cup brown sugar

Dash salt

1 cup creamy peanut butter

1 teaspoon vanilla extract

1. Grease a 9-x-9-inch baking pan, and set aside.

2. Place the corn syrup, brown sugar, and salt in a large saucepan, and bring to a full boil over high heat, stirring constantly. Boil for 1 minute.

3. Stir the peanut butter and vanilla extract into the saucepan, and remove the pan from the heat.

4. Add the jar ingredients to the saucepan, and stir well to combine. Evenly spread the mixture in the prepared pan.

5. Chill for 1 hour before cutting into bars. Serve immediately, or store in an airtight container in the refrigerator for up to 1 week.

CREATING THE JAR

1 cup corn flakes

1 cup semisweet chocolate chips

2 cups crisped rice cereal

1. Wash and thoroughly dry a 1-quart wide-mouth canning jar.

2. Layer the ingredients in the jar as shown at left, pressing firmly with a flat-bottomed object, such as a tart tamper or the bottom of a narrow glass, after each addition. Make the layers as level as possible.

3. Secure the lid, and decorate as desired. (See page 22.) Attach the instructions for making the cookies found below.

Yield: 9 bars

In addition to the contents of the jar, you will need to add the following ingredients:

½ cup light corn syrup

¼ cup brown sugar

Dash salt

1 cup creamy peanut butter

1 teaspoon vanilla extract

Mom's Breakfast Bars

Place the corn syrup, brown sugar, and salt in a large saucepan, and bring to a full boil over high heat, stirring constantly. Boil for 1 minute. Then stir in the peanut butter and vanilla extract, and remove from the heat. Stir all of the jar ingredients into the saucepan. Spread the mixture evenly in a greased 9-x-9-inch baking pan, and chill for 1 hour before cutting into bars. Serve immediately, or refrigerate in an airtight container for up to 1 week.

PURE JOY ALMOND BROWNIES

If you enjoy the famous chocolate, almond, and coconut candy bar,
you will love these brownies.

YIELD:
2 DOZEN BROWNIES

JAR INGREDIENTS

2 1/4 cups sugar

1 1/4 cups all-purpose
flour

3/4 cup coarsely
chopped almonds

1/2 cup unsweetened
cocoa powder

1 teaspoon baking
powder

1 teaspoon salt

ADDITIONAL
INGREDIENTS

3/4 cup melted butter,
slightly cooled

4 eggs

1 teaspoon almond
extract

1 1/4 cups sweetened
flaked coconut

1. Preheat the oven to 350°F. Grease a 13-x-9-inch baking pan, and set aside.

2. Place all of the jar ingredients in a medium-sized bowl, and stir until well combined. Set aside.

3. Place the butter, eggs, and almond extract in a large bowl, and blend well with a spoon.

4. Add the dry ingredients, including the coconut, to the butter mixture, and stir until well combined.

5. Spread the batter evenly in the prepared pan and bake for 20 to 25 minutes, or until the edges are light brown in color.

6. Cool completely in the pan before cutting into bars. Serve immediately, or store in an airtight container for up to 1 week.

CREATINGTHEJAR

¾ cup coarsely chopped almonds

½ cup unsweetened cocoa powder

2 ¼ cups sugar

1 teaspoon baking powder

1 teaspoon salt

1 ¼ cups all-purpose flour

1. Wash and thoroughly dry a 1-quart wide-mouth canning jar.

2. Layer the ingredients in the jar as shown at left, pressing firmly with a flat-bottomed object, such as a tart tamper or the bottom of a narrow glass, after each addition. Make the layers as level as possible.

3. Secure the lid, and decorate as desired. (See page 22.) Attach the instructions for making the cookies found below.

Yield:
2 dozen brownies

In addition to the contents of the jar, you will need to add the following ingredients:

¾ cup melted butter, slightly cooled

4 eggs

1 teaspoon almond extract

1 ¼ cups sweetened flaked coconut

PURE JOY ALMOND BROWNIES

Preheat the oven to 350°F. In a large bowl, combine the melted butter, eggs, and almond extract. Add the contents of the jar and the coconut, and stir until well mixed. Pour the batter into a greased 13-x-9-inch baking pan and bake for 20 to 25 minutes, or until the edges are light brown in color. Cool completely in the pan before cutting into bars. Serve immediately, or store in an airtight container for up to 1 week.

SANDCASTLEBROWNIES

*The layering of the ingredients in this jar reminds me
of colored sand layered in glass bottles.
And the brownies themselves are absolutely scrumptious.*

**YIELD:
2 DOZEN BROWNIES**

JAR INGREDIENTS

2 1/4 cups sugar

1 1/4 cups all-purpose
flour

2/3 cup unsweetened
cocoa powder

1 teaspoon baking
powder

1 teaspoon salt

**ADDITIONAL
INGREDIENTS**

3/4 cup butter,
softened

4 eggs

1. Preheat the oven to 350°F. Grease a 13-x-9-inch baking pan, and set aside.

2. Place all of the jar ingredients in a medium-sized bowl, and stir until well combined. Set aside.

3. Place the butter and eggs in a large bowl, and cream with an electric mixer set on low speed or with a fork.

4. Add the dry ingredients to the butter mixture, and blend with a mixer set on low speed or with a spoon until well combined.

5. Spread the batter evenly in the prepared pan and bake for 20 to 25 minutes, or until the edges are light brown in color.

6. Cool completely in the pan before cutting into bars. Serve immediately, or store in an airtight container for up to 1 week.

CREATING THE JAR

2/3 cup unsweetened cocoa powder

2 1/4 cups sugar

1 teaspoon salt

1 teaspoon baking powder

1 1/4 cups all-purpose flour

1. Wash and thoroughly dry a 1-quart wide-mouth canning jar.

2. Layer the ingredients in the jar as shown at left, pressing firmly with a flat-bottomed object, such as a tart tamper or the bottom of a narrow glass, after each addition. Make the layers as level as possible.

3. Secure the lid, and decorate as desired. (See page 22.) Attach the instructions for making the cookies found below.

SANDCASTLE BROWNIES

Yield:
2 dozen brownies

In addition to the contents of the jar, you will need to add the following ingredients:

3/4 cup butter, softened

4 eggs

Preheat the oven to 350°F. In a large bowl, cream the butter and eggs. Add the contents of the jar, and stir until well mixed. Pour the batter into a greased 13-x-9-inch baking pan and bake for 20 to 25 minutes, or until the edges are light brown in color. Cool completely in the pan before cutting into bars. Serve immediately, or store in an airtight container for up to 1 week.

S'MORE BARS

*Bake a batch of these bars, gather around the fireplace,
and share childhood memories.*

**YIELD:
9 BARS**

JAR INGREDIENTS

1 1/2 cups miniature
marshmallows

1 1/2 cups graham
cracker crumbs

1 cup milk chocolate
chips

1/3 cup brown sugar

**ADDITIONAL
INGREDIENTS**

1/2 cup melted butter,
slightly cooled

1 teaspoon vanilla
extract

1. Preheat the oven to 350°F. Grease a 9-x-9-inch baking pan, and set aside.

2. Place all of the jar ingredients in a large bowl, and stir until well combined.

3. Pour the butter and vanilla extract over the dry ingredients, and mix with a spoon until well combined.

4. Press the dough lightly into the prepared pan, using the back of a fork, and bake for 12 to 15 minutes, or until the top is light brown in color.

5. Cool completely in the pan before cutting into bars. Serve immediately, or store in an airtight container for up to 1 week.

CREATING THE JAR

1½ cups miniature
marshmallows

1 cup milk chocolate
chips

⅓ cup brown sugar

1½ cups graham cracker
crumbs

1. Wash and thoroughly dry a 1-quart wide-mouth canning jar.

2. Layer the ingredients in the jar as shown at left, pressing firmly with a flat-bottomed object, such as a tart tamper or the bottom of a narrow glass, after each addition. Make the layers as level as possible.

3. Secure the lid, and decorate as desired. (See page 22.) Attach the instructions for making the cookies found below.

Yield:
9 bars

In addition to the contents of the jar, you will need to add the following ingredients:

½ cup melted butter, slightly cooled

1 teaspoon vanilla extract

S'MORE BARS

Preheat the oven to 350°F. Place the contents of the jar in a large bowl, and stir until well mixed. Pour the butter and vanilla extract over the dry ingredients, and stir to mix. Press the dough lightly into a greased 9-x-9-inch baking pan, using the back of a fork, and bake for 12 to 15 minutes, or until the top is light brown in color. Cool completely in the pan before cutting into bars. Serve immediately, or store in an airtight container for up to 1 week.

TOFFEE**CRUNCH**BARS

Similar to old-fashioned toffee candy,
these "bars" are simply broken into bite-sized pieces and gobbled up.

YIELD:
12 SERVINGS

JAR INGREDIENTS

2 cups all-purpose
flour

I cup brown sugar

I cup semisweet
chocolate chips

1/2 cup coarsely
chopped almonds

1/4 teaspoon salt

ADDITIONAL
INGREDIENTS

I cup butter, softened

I egg yolk

I teaspoon almond
extract

1/2 teaspoon vanilla
extract

1. Preheat the oven to 350°F.

2. Place all of the jar ingredients in a medium-sized bowl, and stir until well combined. Set aside.

3. Place the butter, egg yolk, and almond and vanilla extracts in a large bowl, and cream with an electric mixer set on low speed or with a fork.

4. Add the dry ingredients to the butter mixture, and mix with a spoon until well combined.

5. Spread the batter evenly in an ungreased 15-x-10-inch jelly roll pan and bake for 20 to 25 minutes, or until hard and golden brown in color. Cool completely in the pan before breaking into pieces.

6. Serve immediately, or store in an airtight container for up to 1 week.

CREATING THE JAR

½ cup coarsely chopped almonds

1 cup semisweet chocolate chips

¼ teaspoon salt

2 cups all-purpose flour

1 cup brown sugar

1. Wash and thoroughly dry a 1-quart wide-mouth canning jar.

2. Layer the ingredients in the jar as shown at left, pressing firmly with a flat-bottomed object, such as a tart tamper or the bottom of a narrow glass, after each addition. Make the layers as level as possible.

3. Secure the lid, and decorate as desired. (See page 22.) Attach the instructions for making the cookies found below.

Yield: 12 servings

In addition to the contents of the jar, you will need to add the following ingredients:

1 cup butter, softened

1 egg yolk

1 teaspoon almond extract

½ teaspoon vanilla extract

TOFFEE CRUNCH BARS

Preheat the oven to 350°F. In a large bowl, cream the butter, egg yolk, and almond and vanilla extracts. Add the contents of the jar, and stir until well mixed. Pour the batter into an ungreased 15-x-10-inch jelly roll pan and bake for 20 to 25 minutes, or until hard and golden brown in color. Cool completely in the pan before breaking into pieces. Serve immediately, or store in an airtight container for up to 1 week.

TROPICAL DELIGHT BARS

*One bite of these easy-to-make bars
and you'll be back for seconds.*

YIELD:
2 DOZEN BARS

JAR INGREDIENTS

2 cups all-purpose
flour

2 cups sweetened
flaked coconut

$^1/_2$ cup brown sugar

$^1/_2$ cup semisweet
chocolate chips

$^1/_2$ cup chopped
almonds

$^1/_4$ teaspoon salt

**ADDITIONAL
INGREDIENTS**

I cup butter, softened

I teaspoon vanilla
extract

1. Preheat the oven to 325°F. Grease a 13-x-9-inch baking pan, and set aside.

2. Place all of the jar ingredients in a medium-sized bowl, and stir until well combined. Set aside.

3. Place the butter and vanilla extract in a large bowl, and cream with an electric mixer set on low speed or with a fork.

4. Add the dry ingredients to the butter mixture, and mix with a spoon until well combined. The batter will be dry and crumbly.

5. Evenly press the batter into the prepared pan using the bottom of a wooden spoon and bake for 25 to 30 minutes, or until the edges are light brown in color.

6. Cool completely in the pan before cutting into bars. Serve immediately, or store in an airtight container for up to 1 week.

CREATINGTHEJAR

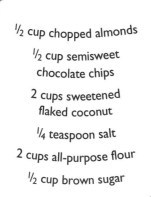

½ cup chopped almonds

½ cup semisweet chocolate chips

2 cups sweetened flaked coconut

¼ teaspoon salt

2 cups all-purpose flour

½ cup brown sugar

1. Wash and thoroughly dry a 1-quart wide-mouth canning jar.

2. Layer the ingredients in the jar as shown at left, pressing firmly with a flat-bottomed object, such as a tart tamper or the bottom of a narrow glass, after each addition. Make the layers as level as possible.

3. Secure the lid, and decorate as desired. (See page 22.) Attach the instructions for making the cookies found below.

Yield:
2 dozen bars

In addition to the contents of the jar, you will need to add the following ingredients:

1 cup butter, softened

1 teaspoon vanilla extract

TROPICAL DELIGHT BARS

Preheat the oven to 325°F. In a large bowl, cream the butter and vanilla extract. Add the contents of the jar, and stir until well mixed. The batter will be dry and crumbly. Press the batter into a greased 13-x-9-inch pan and bake for 25 to 30 minutes, or until the edges are light brown in color. Cool completely in the pan before cutting into bars. Serve immediately, or store in an airtight container for up to 1 week.

Metric Conversion Tables

Common Liquid Conversions

Measurement	=	Milliliters
1/4 teaspoon	=	1.25 milliliters
1/2 teaspoon	=	2.50 milliliters
3/4 teaspoon	=	3.75 milliliters
1 teaspoon	=	5.00 milliliters
1 1/4 teaspoons	=	6.25 milliliters
1 1/2 teaspoons	=	7.50 milliliters
1 3/4 teaspoons	=	8.75 milliliters
2 teaspoons	=	10.0 milliliters
1 tablespoon	=	15.0 milliliters
2 tablespoons	=	30.0 milliliters

Measurement	=	Liters
1/4 cup	=	0.06 liters
1/2 cup	=	0.12 liters
3/4 cup	=	0.18 liters
1 cup	=	0.24 liters
1 1/4 cups	=	0.30 liters
1 1/2 cups	=	0.36 liters
2 cups	=	0.48 liters
2 1/2 cups	=	0.60 liters
3 cups	=	0.72 liters
3 1/2 cups	=	0.84 liters
4 cups	=	0.96 liters
4 1/2 cups	=	1.08 liters
5 cups	=	1.20 liters
5 1/2 cups	=	1.32 liters

Conversion Formulas

LIQUID		
When You Know	Multiply By	To Determine
teaspoons	5.0	milliliters
tablespoons	15.0	milliliters
fluid ounces	30.0	milliliters
cups	0.24	liters
pints	0.47	liters
quarts	0.95	liters

WEIGHT		
When You Know	Multiply By	To Determine
ounces	28.0	grams
pounds	0.45	kilograms

Converting Fahrenheit to Celsius

Fahrenheit	=	Celsius
200–205	=	95
220–225	=	105
245–250	=	120
275	=	135
300–305	=	150
325–330	=	165
345–350	=	175
370–375	=	190
400–405	=	205
425–430	=	220
445–450	=	230
470–475	=	245
500	=	260

Index

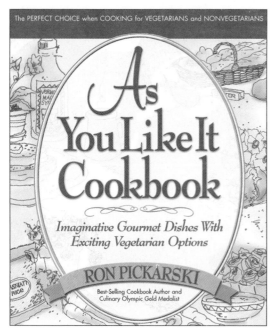

AS YOU LIKE IT COOKBOOK

Imaginative Gourmet Dishes with Exciting Vegetarian Options

Ron Pickarski

When it comes to food, we certainly like to have it our way. However, catering to individual tastes can pose quite a challenge for the cook. Have you ever prepared a wonderful dish, but because it contained beef or chicken, your daughter-in-law, the vegetarian, wouldn't go near it? To meet the challenge of cooking for vegetarians and nonvegetarians alike, celebrated chef Ron Pickarski has written the *As You Like It Cookbook.*

Designed to help you find the perfect meals for today's contemporary lifestyles, the *As You Like It Cookbook* offers over 175 great-tasting dishes that cater to a broad range of tastes. Many of the easy-to-follow recipes are already vegetarian—and offer ingredient alternatives for meat eaters. Conversely, recipes that include meat, poultry, or fish offer nonmeat ingredient options. Furthermore, if the recipe includes eggs or dairy products, a vegan alternative is given for those who follow a strictly plant-based diet. This book has it all—delicious breakfast favorites, satisfying soups and sandwiches, mouth-watering entrées and side dishes, and delectable desserts.

So don't despair the next time someone asks what's for dinner. With the *As You Like It Cookbook,* a tantalizing meal—cooked exactly as your family likes it—is just minutes away.

$16.95 • 216 pages • 7.5 x 9-inch quality paperback • 8 Full-Color pages • ISBN 0-7570-0013-4

Kitchen Quickies
Great, Satisfying Meals in Minutes
Marie Caratozzolo and Joanne Abrams

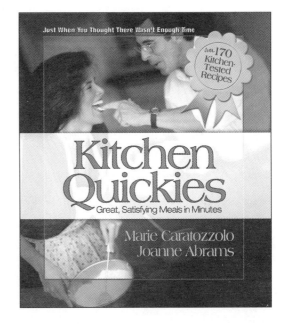

Have you ever left work after a long, hard day feeling totally exhausted, but knowing that the second you arrive home, you have to make a meal, *fast*? Or maybe you've spent the day driving your kids from soccer practice to play dates. Now everyone's clamoring for dinner. But is it possible to get a home-cooked meal on the table before, say, midnight? Absolutely!

The authors of *Kitchen Quickies* know that in this busy world, you just don't have time for hours of grocery shopping followed by hours of food preparation. Their solution? To begin with, virtually all of their over 170 kitchen-tested recipes call for a maximum of five ingredients other than kitchen staples. This makes shopping easier. Then the dish itself takes at most forty-five minutes to prepare. And these delicious dishes are actually good for you—low in fat and high in nutrients!

Kitchen Quickies begins by guiding you through the basics of quick-and-easy cooking. Following this are ten spectacular chapters filled with exciting and imaginative dishes, including sensational soups, satisfying sandwiches, refreshing salads, fabulous pastas, tempting chicken and turkey dishes, sizzling seafood, hearty beef and pork fare, meatless delights, enticing vegetable and grain side dishes, and luscious desserts. In *Kitchen Quickies,* you'll learn how to make tangy Margarita Chicken, Savory Crab Cakes, saucy Penne from Heaven, and more—all in no time flat!

So the next time you think that there's simply no time to cook a good meal, pick up *Kitchen Quickies.* Who knows? You may even have time for a few quickies of your own.

$14.95 • 240 pages • 7.5 x 9-inch quality paperback • 2-Color • 16 Full-Color pages • ISBN 0-7570-0085-1

CONFESSIONS OF A COFFEE BEAN

The Complete Guide to Coffee Cuisine
Marie Nadine Antol

Yes, I have a few things to confess. But before I start, I just want you to know that I couldn't help it. It just happened. Everywhere I went, they wanted me. Now, I have a few things to share—I think it's time to spill the beans.

With a distinct aroma and an irresistible flavor, it has commanded the attention of the world. It is the coffee bean, and while many seek its pleasures, few know its secrets—the secrets of its origin and its appeal, and the key to getting the best out of the bean. Designed for lovers of coffee everywhere, here is a complete guide to understanding and enjoying this celebrated object of our affection.

Part One of Confessions of a Coffee Bean opens with the history of coffee and details the coffee bean's epic journey from crop to cup. It then describes the intriguing evolution of the coffeehouse, highlights surprising facts about coffee and your health, and provides an introduction to the most enticing coffees available today. Finally, this section presents everything you need to know about making a great cup of coffee, from selecting the beans to brewing a perfect pot.

Part Two is a tempting collection of recipes for both coffee drinks and coffee accompaniments. First, you'll learn to make a wide variety of coffee beverages, from steaming brews like Café au Lait to icy concoctions like the Espresso Shake. Then, you'll enjoy a bevy of desserts and other coffee companions, from classic crumb-topped cakes to coffee-kissed creations such as Rich Coffee Tiramisu. You'll even find recipes for coffee-laced candies and sauces.

Whether you're a true coffee aficionado or just someone who loves a good cup of java, this is a book that will entrance you with fascinating facts about all things coffee.

$13.95 • 204 pages • 7.5 x 7.5-inch quality paperback • 2-Color • 0-7570-0020-7

THE SOPHISTICATED OLIVE

The Complete Guide to Olive Cuisine

Marie Nadine Antol

Simple. Elegant. Refined. It has truly evolved into a most sophisticated food. It is the olive. With a history as old as the Bible, the humble olive has matured into a culinary treasure. Enter any fine restaurant and there you will find the sumptuous flavor of olives in cocktails, appetizers, salads, entrées, and so much more. Now, food writer Marie Nadine Antol has created an informative guide to this glorious fruit's many healthful benefits, surprising uses, and spectacular tastes.

Part One of *The Sophisticated Olive* begins by exploring the rich and fascinating history and lore of the olive—from its Greek and Roman legends to its many biblical citations to its place in the New World. It then looks at the olive plant and its range of remarkable properties, covering its uses as a beauty enhancer and a health provider. The book goes on to describe the many varieties of olives that are found around the world, examining their oils, flavors, and interesting characteristics. Part One concludes by providing you with everything you need to know to grow your own olive tree—just like Thomas Jefferson.

Part Two offers over one hundred kitchen-tested recipes designed to put a smile on the face of any olive lover. It first explains the many ways olives can be cured at home. It then covers a host of salads, dressings, tapenades and spreads, soups, side dishes, entrées, breads, cakes, and, of course, beverages to wind down with. So whether you are an olive aficionado or just a casual olive eater, we know you'll be pleased to discover the many new faces of *The Sophisticated Olive*.

$12.95 • 204 pages • 7.5 x 7.5-inch quality paperback • 2-Color • ISBN 0-7570-0024-X

THE MASON JAR SOUP-TO-NUTS COOKBOOK
How to Create Mason Jar Recipe Mixes
Lonnette Parks

Walk into any gift or gourmet store, and you'll see that the popularity of beautiful Mason Jar mixes continues to grow. In this follow-up to her best-selling book, *The Mason Jar Cookie Cookbook,* author and cook extraordinaire Lonnette Parks presents recipes for more than fifty delicious soups, muffins, breads, cakes, pancakes, beverages, and more. And, just as in her previous book, the author tells you how to give the gift of home cooking to friends and family.

For each Mason jar creation, the author provides the full recipe so that you can cook and bake a variety of delights at home. In addition, she includes complete instructions for beautifully arranging the nonperishable ingredients in a Mason jar so that you can give the jar—complete with preparation instructions—to a friend. By adding just a few common ingredients, your friend can then prepare mouthwatering baked goods, refreshing beverages, and satisfying soups and breakfast dishes in a matter of minutes. Recipes include Golden Cornbread, Chocolate Biscotti, Ginger Spice Muffins, Apple-Cinnamon Pancakes, Barley Rice Stew, Viennese Coffee, and much, much more.

Whether you're interested in cooking a stack of golden pancakes in your own kitchen, giving distinctive Mason jar recipe mixes to friends and family, or searching for a clever fund-raising idea, *The Mason Jar Soup-to-Nuts Cookbook* is the perfect book.

$12.95 • 144 pages • 7.5 x 7.5-inch quality paperback • 2-Color • ISBN 0-7570-0129-7

**For more information about our books,
visit our website at www.squareonepublishers.com**